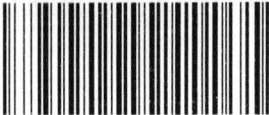

Relax

Interiors for Human Wellness

Introduction by Karim Rashid

Frame Publishers
Amsterdam

Birkhäuser
Basel·Boston·Berlin

Contents

022

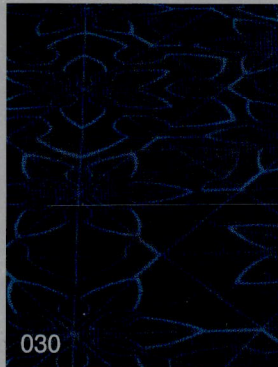

030

038

046

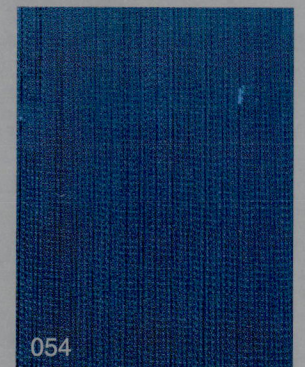

054

100

108

116

124

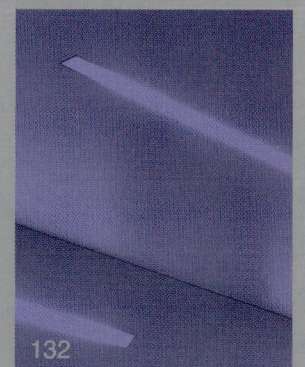

132

180

186

194

202

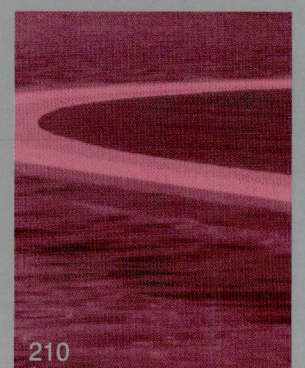

210

gyms

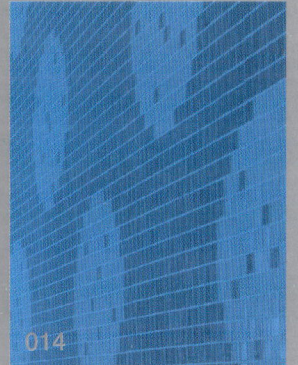

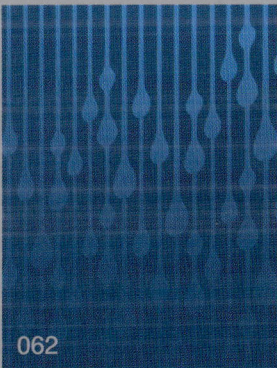

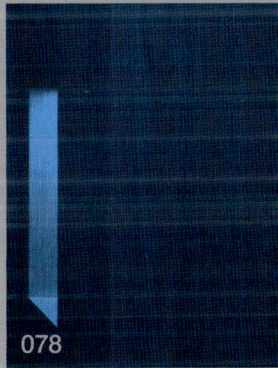

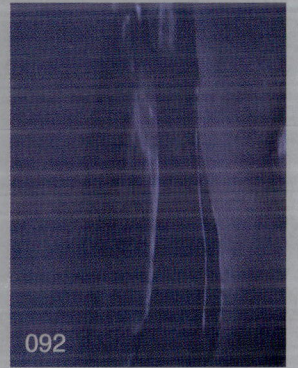

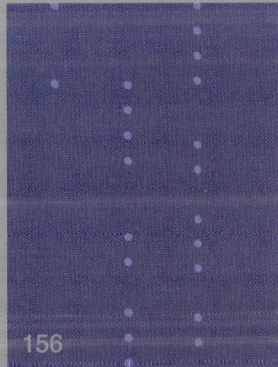

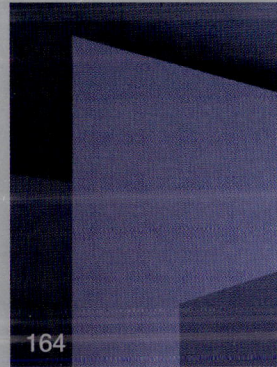

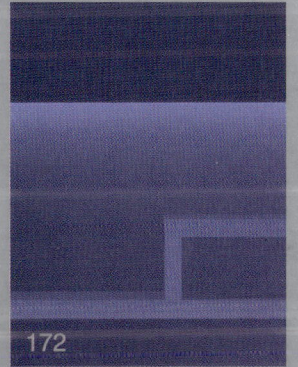

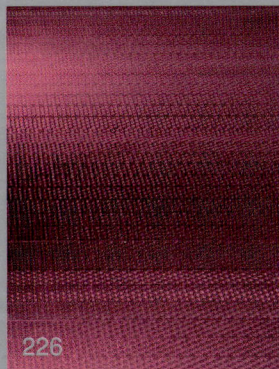

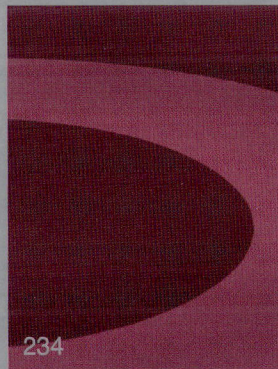

006

014

062

070

078

086

092

140

148

156

164

172

218

226

234

242

250

Section 01

Spas

Text by Karim Rashid

'Forever young, I want to be forever young'
Alphaville, 1983

I want to live forever. We all do. But we know all too well that we are mortal, that time on this planet is temporary, and that this evanescent life can carry, at times, momentary pleasures of hedonism, of pleasure-seeking rituals, and of complete physical and spiritual bliss. Engrossed in our sensorial experiences, we accept physical pleasure as a natural need, as very much part of primordial human desire. With the new information age and full-on global capitalism, we are working more than ever before in history and leaving little time for ourselves. The average workweek in America is 56 hours and in Japan 59 hours (up from 34 hours in the 1970s). This trend is moving across the planet. For the sake of balance and repose, the spa phenomenon is paramount, and every day we see the opening of new spas that are meeting the demands and needs of our hectic, stress-bombarded information age. Splurging for the purpose of 'treating oneself' as a reward for a tumultuous, exhaustive schedule has led to the creation of spas as omnipresent oases of luxury. You can opt for treatments costing into the thousands of dollars for a day. In fact, a massage is not enough any more. Tourists and businesspeople frequently spend several hours receiving all kinds of treatments to combat stress. Last year, seven of the top ten Christmas gifts in North America were immaterial to one degree or another: from video games to digital music and software, from DVDs to gift certificates for food and, not least, for spa treatments. Hence the demand for new spas and, in turn – since we live in the midst of a new era of enlightenment in terms of design – the development

of spas that are becoming more contemporary, more interesting, and more alternative in décor and design. We witness on the following pages 'less of the traditional spa' vernacular that used to convince us that health was spiritual and not physical, that it was tied only to nature and not science, and that it reflected Eastern aesthetics of space. Finally, there tends to be a departure from the typical Zen-like aesthetics of places for relaxation, health and wellness. For the longest time, spas have been steeped in semantics of *faux* nature, and now we are witnessing a shift. Today's aesthetics (the word comes from the Greek for 'feeling') are more symbiotic with the new spirit of design, with new materials, new technologies and even 'technorganic' spaces, which communicate a sophisticated technological aspect to our health. There is a new softness, a new casualness, that is apparent in some of the projects in this book.

We no longer want to go to a spa just to relax or to escape. We want to walk out of the spa five years younger; hence the ambience must communicate that desire.

The spa concept should combine the use of advanced therapies and treatments, of new cosmetic innovations and new technologies, with the global trend of seeking perpetual youth.

'Without progress we would still be living only into our 40s, without ambition we would still be living in caves, and without designers we would still be living in a banal, uninspired and inhuman world' «Karim»

client
Loisium Hotelbetrieb
engineers
Retter & Partner and
Altherm Engineering
total floor area (m²)
2800

**duration of
construction**
1.5 years
opening
October 2005

project
Loisium
Loisiumallee 1
3550 Langenlois
Austria
T +43 273 4322 400
F +43 273 4322 4030
info@loisium.at

gps
N 48°28' E 015°40'

Steven Holl Architects

Loisium

langenlois/austria

Text by Anneke Bokern

Wine and wellness were to be combined in the spa of the Loisium Hotel. Steven Holl drew on centuries-old wine cellars beneath Langenlois for the design, borrowed the colour of local wine bottles for the palette, and completed the picture with contemporary, ivory-white furniture.

Langenlois, a small Austrian town marked by baroque architecture, had been experiencing problems with tourism. Although the area produces many good wines, the town and its surroundings were overshadowed by Vienna and by the better-known wine region of Wachau. What's more, to some extent Austrian wines were still carrying the taint of the 1980s glycol scandal. In 2001 Langenlois vintners met and made plans for boosting the image of the town, along with their incomes. Their goal was a new visitors centre to accompany their vineyards, as well as a hotel. The centre, to be called Loisium, would combine two current trends in tourism, wine and wellbeing, thus increasing its appeal as a tourist attraction. The visitors centre opened in early 2005, and the hotel followed in October of the same year. In the hotel spa, guests are pampered with treatments such as the Barrique bath and body wrap, the relaxation bath with grape extract, and a grape-seed-oil massage. Loisium wholeheartedly concurs with the motto: If it tastes good, you can safely apply it to the outside, too. Responsible for the architecture of the entire complex

is Steven Holl Architects. The wine-producing families asked Dietmar Steiner, director of Vienna's Centre for Architecture, for help in selecting firms for an invitational design competition. 'One of the clients had grown up in Helsinki and knew the Kiasma Museum, which we built,' says Holl. The first brief simply requested a design for the visitors centre. 'I had already included a general outline of the hotel in my plans. After our presentation, the mayor of Langenlois said, rather succinctly, "We'll build it. And we'll build the hotel too." The commission was ours.' Holl's point of departure lay beneath the site: labyrinthine wine cellars estimated to be as much as 900 years old. The architect refers to them as 'a second invisible town beneath the actual town of Langenlois'. He based his design of the new spatial structures on the geometry of the old cellars, creating a kind of oenological trinity: cellars 'under the ground', the half-sunken cube that forms the visitors centre 'in the ground', and a hotel 'above the ground'. The hotel is a three-storey solitaire of red, yellow and green, with a brushed-aluminium skin and a glazed ground-floor complex. From a distance, it looks like an

The labyrinthine shape of the lamp above the bar not only resembles the floor plan of the underground wine cellars, but also appears as an inlaid pattern in the floor and ceiling of the Vintage Relax lounge.

angular UFO hovering above the vineyards. Built parallel to the rows of vines, it forms a horseshoe around an inner courtyard, which opens in the direction of the visitors centre. The doors of the main entrance to the hotel lead directly to the foyer, a space that offers the guest three choices: a staircase to the bedrooms; a right turn to the restaurant, bar and lounge; and a left turn across a gently sloping ramp to the 1000-m^2 spa area, which occupies three floors.

The cavern-like rooms of the spa are bathed in jade green or, in wine-country terms, 'bottle green'. Flooring, walls, stone benches and steps are clad in green mosaic tile alternated with dark-brown stained oak. The hotel lobby leads directly into the spa lobby, where guests can access a series of adjoining rooms, including a hair salon, a wet-treatment room and a Vichy shower. Other features are a fitness room and the dual-level Vintage Relax lounge, which is glazed on three sides, offering a panoramic view of the hotel's inner courtyard, as well as surrounding vineyards. At the same time, a central void makes it possible to observe both levels of the Vintage Relax lounge. Fitted furniture and trolleys distributed throughout the spa were designed specially for the Loisium by Austrian designer sha. and made in the Black Forest. In the lounges, ivory-white Peanut benches and chairs by Little Book of Furniture are complemented by the clean lines of occasional tables designed in 1906 by famed Austrian architect Josef Hoffmann and currently reproduced by the Wittmann Carpentry Workshop. Illumination comes from built-in ceiling spots and custom-designed cork pendants by CW.

The result is a spa of an unconventional nature, which playfully improvises on the wine-cellar theme without descending into kitsch. Subterranean spaces, although cavern-like, have a thoroughly modern look thanks to the furnishings. The strongest link between the themes of wine and wellbeing is the green mosaic tiling, which alludes not only to water and wine bottles, but also to the verdure of the vineyards that encompass the complex.

'Old labyrinthine wine cellars are a second invisible town beneath the actual town of Langenlois' «Steven Holl»

Going underground:
bottle-green tiles and custom-
designed cork pendants create
a grotto-like atmosphere
with style.

Upstairs, downstairs:
both floors of Loisium's Vintage
Relax lounge offer a great view of
the vineyards.

architect

Steven Holl Architects
450 West 31st St.,
11th Floor
New York, NY 10001
USA
T +1 212 629 7262
F +1 212 629 7312
mail@stevenholl.com
www.stevenholl.com

photographers

Christian Richters
chrichters@aol.com
-
Margherita Spiluttini
office@spiluttini.com
www.spiluttini.com

legend

01 Lobby
02 Meeting room
03 Hair salon
04 Wet-treatment room
05 Vichy shower
06 Fitness
07 Relaxation room
08 Restaurant
09 Smoking lounge
10 Bar
11 Kitchen
12 Office
13 Lavatories

First floor

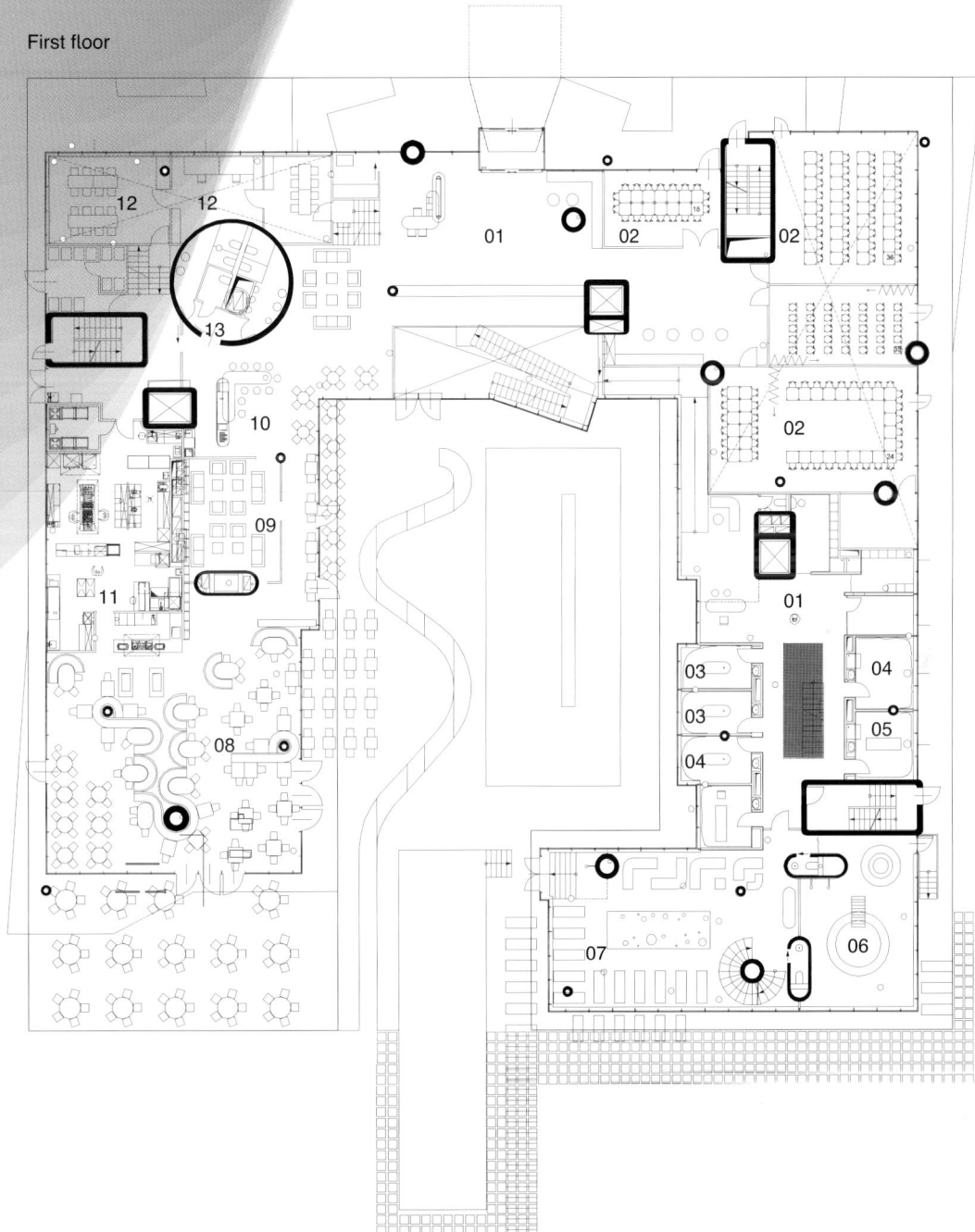

meters 0 1   5   10

N

← Loisium's visitors centre has
  an irregularly faceted metallic
  façade cleft with strategically
  positioned openings that allow
  light to enter the interior.

client
Gesundheitszentrum
Lanserhof
engineer
A3
general planning
Malojer Baumanagement
façade
Raffl Anlagenbau
manufacturer
Spechtenhauser Holz- und
Glasbau

lighting design
Tropp Lighting Design
capacity
3000 clients
total floor area (m²)
1500
total cost (€)
3 million
**duration of
construction**
5 months
opening
December 2005

project
Gesundheitszentrum
Lanserhof
Kochholzweg 153
6072 Lans bei Innsbruck
Austria
T +43 512 3866 60
F +43 512 3782 82
info@lanserhof.at
www.lanserhof.at

gps
N 47°14' E 011°25'

Designstudio Regina Dahmen-Ingenhoven

Gesundheits-zentrum Lanserhof

lans bei innsbruck/austria

Text by Anneke Bokern

'A medical space station, which beams its guests into a healthier life.'
This is how Regina Dahmen-Ingenhoven describes Lanserhof, the new medical
therapeutic centre in the Tyrol that she and her Düsseldorf-based studio
designed. The traditional mountain hotel near Innsbruck has been transformed
into a minimalist space-age temple dedicated to the body. Dr McCoy goes Alpine.

Originally, Lanserhof was a classic Tyrolean hotel decked
out in typical rustic Alpine kitsch. When the present
director took over its management in 1984, a healthy
long-term overhaul of the building was prescribed, one
befitting the 'Lans_Med_Concepts' focus on purifying,
cleansing and detoxifying the body. Over several phases
the interior was redesigned and renovated to become
a model of highly polished minimalism, radiating a
wonderful sense of wellbeing. The latest phase was the
establishment of a medical therapeutic centre, which
opened its doors in early 2006 and covers over 1500 m².

'It must be beautiful' was the succinct yet demanding
challenge presented to the architects. Dahmen-Ingenhoven
was in full agreement with this aim. 'Beauty is highly
important to our daily sense of wellbeing and to our
ethical ideas. If beauty were to disappear from the world,
the world would lose its soul.' Thus we can say that
Lanserhof's guests are transported from their workaday
environment to a completely new setting to refresh their
souls. It is far removed from the traditional Alpine inn
and the overblown grandeur of the luxury hotel.
The architects of the medical therapeutic centre developed

Soft flowing shapes and watery blue tiles characterize the Kneipp Spa at Lanserhof.

an open, fluent spatial design. The island rooms are bathed in minimalist white with a contrasting soft blue. Rounded corners contribute to both the feel-good factor and the space-age theme.

Daylight floods the funnel-shaped health centre through a vast window at the front of the building. Light penetrates the cell-like rooms, which are laid out according to their need for natural light. Doctors' consultation rooms, massage rooms and the lounge are adjacent to the window. Requiring less daylight and situated farther away from the window are reception, pools and treatment rooms. Offices and storerooms are at the rear.

The reception area, at the heart of the facility, leads directly to the main lounge. A large, round, bright-blue sofa fosters communication among the guests, whose gaze is drawn to the view of the mountains through the glass frontage. A photo of the same panoramic view covers a 50-m-long translucent wall that runs parallel to the glazed façade, separating massage and consultation rooms from circulation areas. Entering one of the doors in the wall with the photo, the visitor sees an identical mountain vista, but now through the window. 'We brought nature into the space to establish harmony between outdoors and indoors,' Dahmen-Ingenhoven explains.

Wet areas behind the reception zone include pools, showers and spas. Reflecting the theme of water, they are clad in Bisazza mosaic tiles in various shades of blue. The tiled surfaces mirror the motif of circular holes – seen in the acoustic ceilings, for example – that is repeated in every room, making a purely functional necessity into part of the design. These 'polka dots' bring oxygen bubbles to mind.

Circles also appear in some of the treatment rooms, but as yellow openings of various sizes in the walls,

which are lit from within. Built-in lighting is an important design device at Lanserhof, where all illumination is indirect. Pure white light or coloured light streams out of niches, slits and holes, creating a serene atmosphere. The only conventional lamps to be seen are flush-mounted spots in the acoustic ceilings. All furniture in the medical therapeutic centre was purpose-designed by the Ingenhoven team. Where possible, it has been integrated into the walls, and none of the pieces has hard edges or sharp corners. Soft, natural materials contrast with hard, shiny, high-tech materials: cupboards and counters made from Corian (a blend of natural minerals and acrylic polymer) and Parapan (an even glossier acrylic resin) are juxtaposed with warm oak panelling, Flokati-covered stools and a felt-upholstered sofa in the main lounge.

The so-called 'soft room' is also furnished in white felt. In this mellow, cavern-like interior, six couches with their head ends set into the wall invite guests to lie down and experience light therapy. Flooring in this room and throughout most of the centre is made from seamless white epoxy resin. The exceptions are two shiatsu rooms that resemble monastery cells, which feature walnut flooring that 'represents a close bond with the earth'. Ascetic health regimes, as well as the hippy ethno-aesthetic urging a return to the womb, are long gone. Nowadays, minimalism is linked with the cult of the body. The concept of wellness at Lanserhof chimes with the spirit of the times but is based on 'the latest top-class medical science, along with cross-cultural therapies, supplemented by a delicious gourmet, high-energy diet'. Dahmen-Ingenhoven has succeeded in translating this temporary mix of high tech, luxury and wellbeing into a world of compelling spatial design.

↑ Monastic shiatsu rooms are the only places in the centre with wooden floors.

→ At Lanserhof, light comes from a variety of indirect sources, including the 'polka dots' that Regina Dahmen-Ingenhoven has used to illuminate treatment rooms.

Keeping it cosy: Flokati-covered stools add a touch of warmth to a space featuring cool surfaces in minimalist white.

'A medical space station,
which beams its guests
into a *healthier* life'
«Regina Dahmen-Ingenhoven»

architect
Designstudio Regina
Dahmen-Ingenhoven
project partner
Jan Görgemanns
Plange Mühle 1
40221 Düsseldorf
Germany
T +49 211 30101 01
www.drdi.de
info@drdi.de

photographer
Studio Holger Knauf
hk@holgerknauf.de
www.holgerknauf.de

legend
01 Lounge
02 Consultation area
03 Preparatory room
04 Kneipp Spa Island
05 Massage room
06 Shiatzu room
07 Acupuncture room
08 SPA Jaran
09 Colon-hydro room
10 Agescan laboratory
11 Pool and shower
12 Hydromassage
13 Gymnastic room
14 Treatment room
15 Liquid energy
16 Doctors office
17 Chill-out area
18 Staff room
19 Lavatories
20 Storage

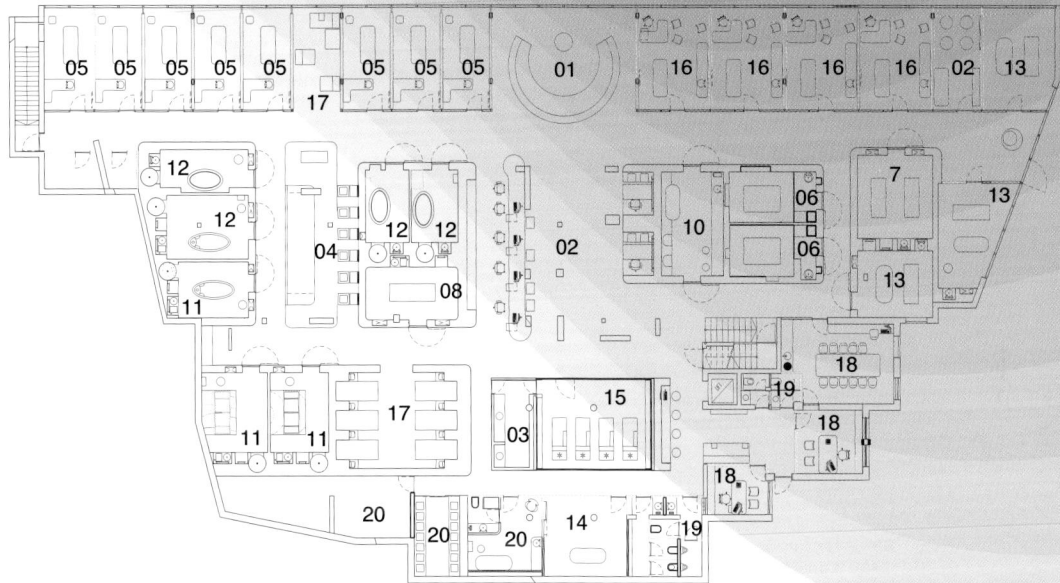

↖ The lounge offers a panoramic
view of the Alps, and an identical
vista appears on wallpaper in the
adjoining corridor.

← Space-age cubicles in blue and
white create an atmosphere of
privacy for chats between guests
and consultants.

client
Tschuggen Hotel Group
spa specialist
Klafs (Mr Burkhardt Geipel,
Mr Andreas Erke)
consultant
Fanzun
engineers
Fanzun, Klafs, Bühler
+ Scherler and Hans
Hermann

total floor area (m²)
5000
**duration of
construction**
3 summer periods
opening
December 2006

project
Tschuggen Grand Hotel
7050 Arosa
Switzerland
T +41 81 378 9999
F +41 81 378 9990
bergoase@tschuggen.ch
www.tschuggen.ch

gps
N 47°28' E 008°18'

Mario Botta
Tschuggen Bergoase
arosa/switzerland

Text by Stephan Ott

The Swiss canton of Graubünden is famous for its exclusive ski resorts. Arosa, which numbers among Graubünden's illustrious circle of chic destinations, gained a new wellness facility in December 2006. Tschuggen Bergoase, designed by Mario Botta, is fully integrated into the town's mountainous landscape.

The Tschuggen Grand Hotel in Arosa, Switzerland, began life in 1883 as a tuberculosis sanatorium and was converted to a prestigious hotel only when Arosa became a ski resort. After a fire destroyed the hotel in 1966, it was rebuilt in '60s style and reopened in 1970. Over 60 million Swiss francs have been invested in its renovation since April 2004. Since once again reopening at the end of 2006, the hotel offers guests luxurious surroundings and an extraordinary wellness facility.

These days, as snowfall becomes more and more unpredictable, smart Swiss hoteliers are offering attractive alternatives to winter sports. The Tschuggen Grand Hotel sees a bright future in two seasons opening accommodation. Influencing the decision of the Tschuggen Grand Hotel (TGH) to furnish guests with wellness and spa facilities was the rising demand for therapies and treatment packages aimed at good health and a sense of wellbeing. The group elected to build a wellness centre that would be unsurpassed in terms of architecture, design, equipment and furnishings. Setting a new standard was a budget of 35 million Swiss francs

– more than half of the aforementioned investment – for Bergoase alone, making the centre in Arosa one of the larger European developments in the field of wellness. Renowned architect and designer Mario Botta, who hails from Lugano, Switzerland, was commissioned to design Bergoase. He approached the task armed with the conviction 'to build without overbuilding'. He didn't want an enormous structure that would perch on the landscape, so to speak, but a complex that would be fully integrated into the mountainous environment and do nothing to disrupt the magnificent view of its natural surroundings. He saw the symbiosis between building and landscape as a goal to be realized through a major and highly concrete operation. After part of the mountain slope had been excavated, some of the rock that had been removed was pulverized and used to make cement, an ingredient of the concrete from which the centre was then erected. The remainder of the slope was poured back onto the roof construction and landscaped, concealing part of the Bergoase below.

Nine sail-shaped volumes between 9 and 13 m high rise

↑ All saunas were designed individually by Klafs, geared to the
   architecture and materials of the
   Bergoase.

← Light towers: The sail-shaped
   volumes can be seen from afar.

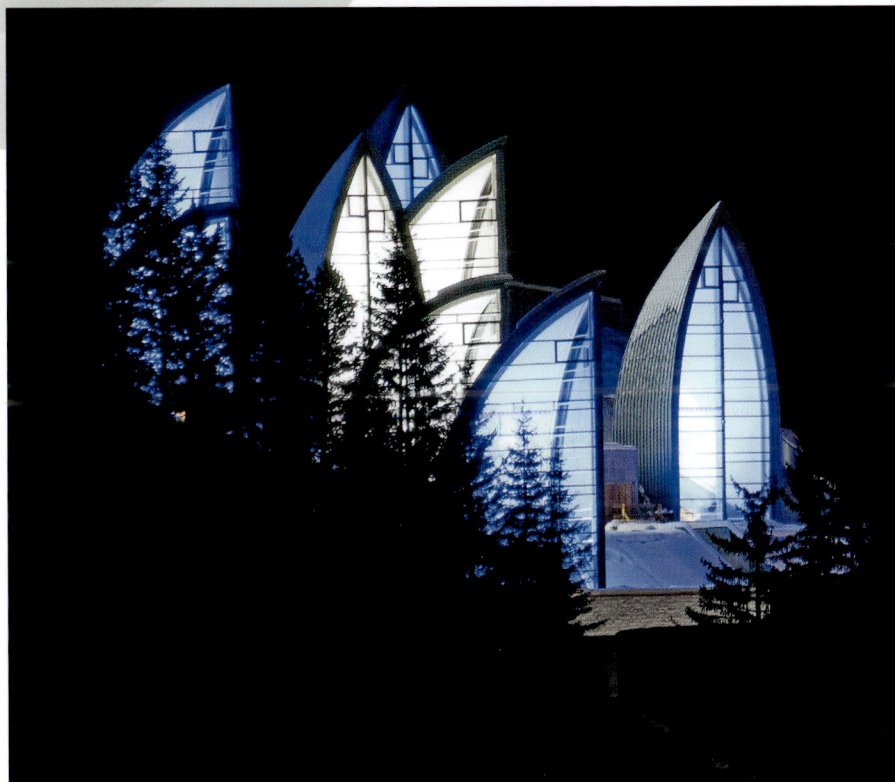

from the base of the building, their windows facing the valley and their rear façades – clad in pre-weathered, slate-grey Rheinzink – facing the mountain. Evocative of trees or leaves, these organic beacons are the more visible symbols of Bergoase. Their technical function is to allow daylight to enter the interior of the oasis, thus minimizing the need for artificial light. An aspect of the design that should not be underestimated, this element illustrates the architect's belief that natural light is indispensable for human wellbeing.

Clarity of form, local building materials and a subtle play of light and shadow characterize Botta's architecture for Bergoase, particularly with respect to the sauna section of the complex. All saunas, steam rooms and relaxation amenities were designed individually yet geared to the architecture and to the materials selected by the architect. It was especially important that TGH hit on the right choice of partners to make the fittings and furnishings for these interiors. They selected Klafs, the renowned sauna and specialists from Schwäbisch-Hall, which lies some 60 km northeast of Stuttgart. As Corinne Denzler, group director at Tschuggen Hotel Group explains: 'Klafs was chosen to realize the spa fittings and furnishings, as the architects and clients were convinced that, as a partner, Klafs could be fully relied upon to meet the demands of the design with their sophisticated techniques. Not just a firm under contract, therefore, Klafs was brought into the planning team of architects and engineering specialists at an early stage.'

Bergoase extends over a total of four levels. The first level accommodates the fitness centre, which boasts the latest generation of fitness equipment. The second is devoted completely to therapy. The third level of Bergoase is connected directly to the Tschuggen Grand Hotel by way of a glass bridge. Housed at this level are saunas, relaxation areas, and the spa restaurant and lounge. Outside Bergoase proper – also set into the slope – is a mountainside sauna with its own fireplace. Botta has created a venue that caters to the hotel's female guests in particular, providing them with a separate area that features a sauna, a steam room, a cooling-down area and relaxation facilities. A convivial lounge area with an open fire and a panoramic view of the spectacular Alpine landscape, together with a silent room, round off the third level's exclusive facilities. Found on the fourth level of Bergoase is a swimming area with indoor and outdoor pools, various bubbling attractions, an aqua gym and a children's paddling pool. Numerous water games relate the cycle of the four seasons.

The symbiosis between building
and landscape was a priority
while designing the Bergoase.

The design illustrates architect Mario Botta's belief
that natural light is *indispensable for human wellbeing*

↑ The showers are part of the cool-cater area.

↖ Clarity of form and a subtle play of light and shadow characterize the architecture.

↑ Cozy: an open fire in one of the relaxation area's.

← The steam bath on the third level caters to the hotel's female guests in particular.

architect
Mario Botta Architetto
Davide Macullo
Via Ciani 16
6904 Lugano
Switzerland
T +41 91 972 8625
F +41 91 970 1454
info@botta.ch
www.botta.ch

photographers
Enrico Cano
enrico.cano@tin.it
www.enricocano.com
-
Foto Homberger
Urs Homberger
info@fotohomberger.ch
www.fotohomberger.ch
-
Pino Musi
pino.musi@alice.it

legend
01 Reception
02 Wardrobe
03 Sauna
04 Steam bath
05 Foot bath
06 Beauty cabin
07 Body-treatment cabin
08 Pool
09 Water feature
10 Terrace
11 Showers
12 Relaxation area
13 Silent room
14 Suite
15 Cool-cater area
16 Storage
17 Pool technical area
18 Mechanical room

First Floor

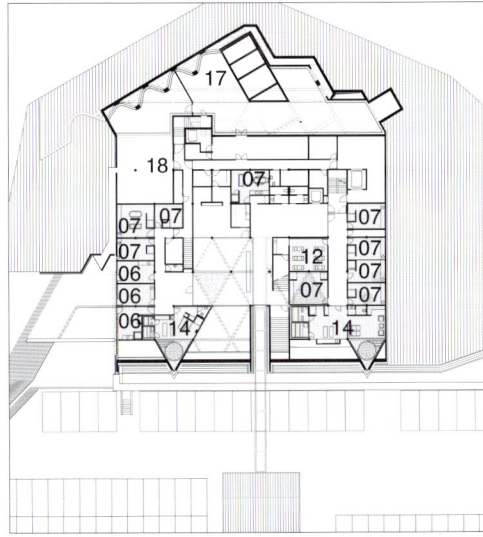

Second Floor

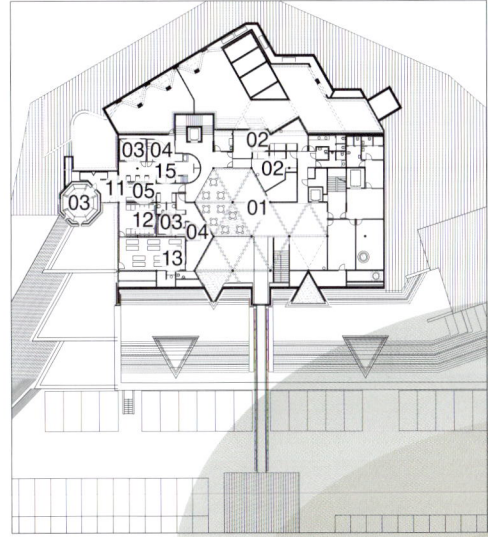

Third Floor

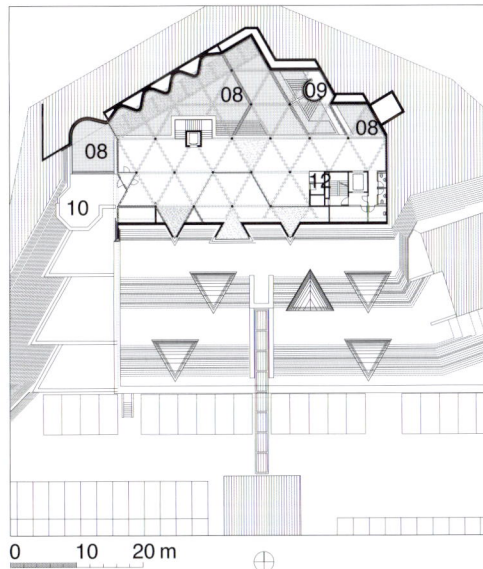

0   10   20 m

client
Genossenschaft Migros
Aare
project management
S+B Baumanagement
project development
rob.d.sein, Roger Bennet
engineers
Enerconom, MBJ
Bauphysik + Akustik,
Schneider Aquatec,
Balplan and Hefti. Hess.
Martignoni

manufacturers
Rosconi, Lädrach Holzbau,
Axima, Claude Bickel,
Schule für Holzbildhauerei
Brienz, Bodanwerft, vonAll-
men and Fetaxid
capacity
Fitness: 400 clients,
Hammam: 80 clients
total floor area (m²)
4000
total cost (€)
11 million
budget per m² (€)
1700

**duration of
construction**
6 months
opening
November 2005
project
Fitnesspark Haman
Brown Boveri Platz 1
5400 Baden
Switzerland
T +41 56 200 0380
F +41 56 200 0381

gps
N 47°28' E 008°18'

Ushi Tamborriello

Fitnesspark Hamam

baden/switzerland

Text by Stephan Ott

Housed in the converted transformer hall of erstwhile electrical-engineering company Brown Boveri & Cie (BBC), the 4000-m² Migros Fitnesspark in Baden offers a full range of facilities for good health and wellbeing, including saunas, massage rooms, solaria and Switzerland's largest and most up-to-date hammam.

Baden, *nomen est omen*, has been attracting visitors to its 18 hot springs not only for centuries but for millennia. Camping in this place they called Aquae Helveticae some 2000 years ago, Roman soldiers enjoyed the benefits of water bubbling from the ground at a comfortable temperature of 47 degrees. Admittedly, Migros Fitnesspark doesn't offer thermal waters bubbling from the ground, but it does have a hammam (Arabic for 'bath'), an oriental ambience and a pleasurable pampering programme, as well as a range of sports facilities. The Migros Cooperative Group, better known outside Switzerland as a supermarket chain, opened its first Fitnesspark in Lucerne in 1977 and has been developing its philosophy of wellbeing and fitness ever since. A recent addition to their network is Fitnesspark Hamam, realized in a converted transformer hall in Baden. Asked to design the ambitious project was a Munich-based team headed by Ushi Tamborriello, whose work covers production design and interior architecture. This team has previously realized the interior design of two other Migros-parks; the Hamam Münstergasse, and Puls 5, both located in Zürich.

Recalling the plan, Tamborriello says her task entailed 'a challenging pair of opposites'. Faced with the design of a fitness park and an oriental bathhouse in a traditional industrial building, she saw 'a contradiction that had to be solved through innovation'.
Dominating the exterior wall on the east side of the building is glazing that has been integrated into the design of the entrance. Inside, visitors are greeted by a entrance café with a counter that leads to the hammam. Throughout the hammam, dark colours accentuated by soft white lights convey a feeling of depth, simplicity and tranquillity. Here the walls are predominately dark green, grey or the colour of raw earth. Materials such as glass – rising from floor to ceiling – and steel refer to the industrial use of the original building. Complementing them are diffuse green lighting and dark wood, which provide the interiors with an air of warmth and security. Floral floor patterns, which enhance the desired atmosphere, are accentuated in the dim light in a mystical and authentic way. 'We repeatedly broke with the classic model on which the hammam is based, in order to reflect

'We repeatedly broke with the classic model on which the hammam is based, in order to *reflect the industrial context and modernity of the site*'

«Ushi Tamborriello»

↑ Inside Fitnesspark Hamam, visitors find no stark reminders of the transformer hall that once operated on this site.

← Floral floor patterns and dim lighting combine to create a mystical atmosphere.

the industrial context and modernity of the site,' says Tamborriello. 'What remains, though, are the mystical spaces that orbit around a singular theme: the celebration of a bathing ritual that soothes body and soul.'

A completely new floor covering was developed for the hammam. This flooring meets the required standards of hygiene, is easy to clean, has a non-slip surface and, last but not least, is an aesthetic addition to the bathing area. Participating in the development and realization of floor patterns for this part of the complex was the Brienz School of Woodcarving.

Although interiors reserved for fitness and wellness are located in a new-build extension to the transformer hall, the same central entrance at the east side of the building lends access to these facilities as well. The spatial structure of the fitness area is largely open and transparent, offering an unrestricted view of the surrounding landscape and providing an ideal ambience for physical exercise. Here, too, the colour scheme and the choice of materials reflect both the history of the building complex and its new function. Colour added to smooth industrial flooring that was originally a shade of anthracite made the surface more suitable for the new environment. A parquet floor in the fitness rooms combines an industrial look with the warmth of wood. Fabrics used in this area are soft and

highly tactile. 'Colour', 'warmth' and 'tactility' are words that describe the entire fitness centre, a place not at all like the majority of sports centres with their hard, white, sterile surfaces.

The interior designer offers a final summary of the fitness park: 'In general, the architecture considers the opposites found in a complex built for fitness and wellness and interprets them through energy, power and movement. Extrovert activities, such as strenuous exercise, take place in spacious rooms that open to the outdoors; here we've used light colours and hard surfaces. Introvert pastimes related to relaxation and wellbeing have been given darker, softer, warmer surroundings. They take place in a world which is focused more on the inner soul, a world with its own unique resources.'

↑   Generally dark and pleasantly ambient colours, emphasized by soft lighting, give the interior a sense of depth, simplicity and calm.

→   The newly developed floor covering meets aesthetic standards, as well as health and safety requirements.

↖ In the reflections, one sees an impressive and ongoing interplay of grey stone walls and moving water.

↑ Green light and dark wood evoke a feeling of warmth and security.

Shape, material, colour and light merge to form a harmonious entity.

interior designer
Ushi Tamborriello, Interior
& Production Design
Holzstrasse 33
80469 Munich
Germany
T +49 170 2156 334
ushi@tamborriello.de
www.tamborriello.de

photographer
Jochen Splett
Jochen.splett@t-online.de
www.jochensplett.de

legend
01 Reception
02 Lobby
03 Cloakroom
04 Meditation bath
05 Exercise bath
06 Steam bath
07 Foot bath
08 Sauna
09 Sicaklik
10 Massage room
11 Purgation room
12 Rhassoul
13 Meditation room
14 Relaxation room
15 Café Hamam
16 Mechanical systems

Ground floor - Hammam

First basement – Wellness

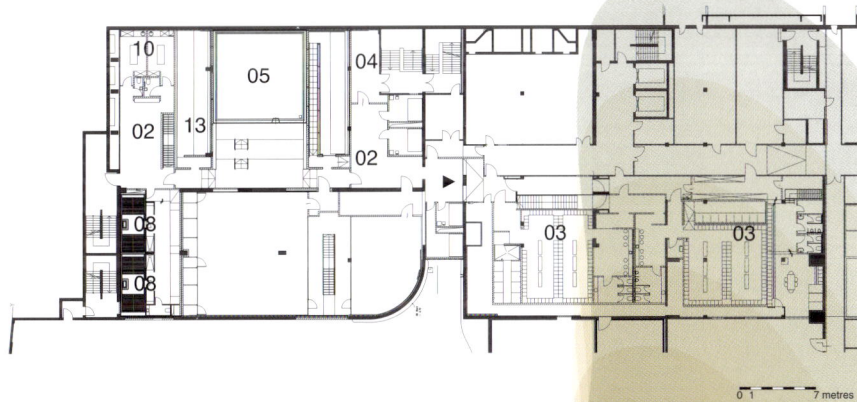

Second basement – Wellness

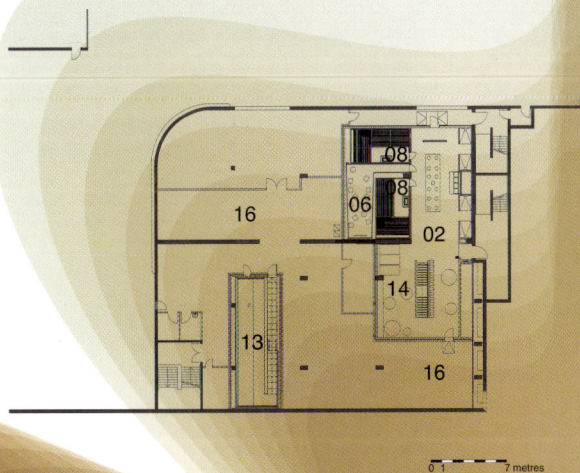

client
COLA Holdings
engineer
Gilbert Jackomy
manufacturer
CPMG Menuiserie
total floor area (m²)
1700
total cost (€)
4 million

budget per m²
2400
**duration of
construction**
8 months
opening
October 2006

project
L'Espace Payot
62 Rue Pierre Charron
75008 Paris
France
T +33 145 6142 08
F +33 145 6124 06
info-espacepayot@payot.fr
www.payot.com

gps
N 48°52' E 002°18'

Joseph Caspari
L'Espace Payot
paris/france

Text by Tim Groen

For the basement of a 19th-century building on a street adjacent to the Champs-Elysées, sculptor and architect Joseph Caspari designed a minimalist spa *par excellence.* Shunning luxury of the flashy kind, L'Espace Payot combines physical indulgences with timeless architecture.

'There was no briefing from the client,' says Caspari, 'I made the space according to my idea of what a luxurious spa, pool and fitness space should look like.' The architect and his client, who is a property developer, met at an exhibition of sculptures by Caspari. The former bought one of the latter's sculptures, and the two became friends. Caspari says that when their friendship led to an architecture commission, 'my client trusted me with what was his first project involving a spa, as well as my own'. Interestingly, it was only after the spa had been designed that the developer and cosmetics firm Payot determined the exact usage of interior spaces spread over two floors. The overall inspiration for Caspari's concept was the 'stone and water architecture' of Roman thermae and classic Turkish baths. The use of contrasting white marble from Carrare and grey granite from Cardoso – installed by a highly specialized team from Portugal – refers to the sensation caused by moving from the ground floor, illuminated by daylight, to the relative darkness of the underground spaces. 'Because of the unavailability of natural light for the subterranean zone,' says Caspari, 'I created an atmosphere that relies on invisible sources of changing lights.'
The entire spa – cabins, pool and hammam – is equipped with an installation of multicolour light-emitting

diodes (LEDs). In the treatment cabins, also referred to as 'cubicles', the colour of the light corresponds to the type of treatment provided in each cabin. In the rest of the interior at L'Espace Payot, all colour changes in the lighting are computerized.
Guests enter the ground-floor reception area, which together with its white marble cube sets the tone for their visit, before descending to the lower level. 'I limited myself to three materials: marble, granite and oak,' says Caspari. 'I attempted to use them in an organic way to avoid any decorative elements or effects.' The underground swimming pool, positioned at the centre of the floor, is crossed by a footbridge that leads to the gymnasium, a space referred to as the 'Chamber of Mirrors'. Situated behind a mirrored door are the wet areas of the sauna and the rounded hammam, which is the only nonlinear element in the entire project. A large hallway, whose floor is dotted with rows of built-in halogen lamps, ends at an area featuring beauty-treatment cubicles with cool, marble-surfaced exteriors that contrast with interiors panelled in warm, light-coloured oak.
'The design of the cubicles,' says Caspari, 'is dictated by their specific functions.' He goes on to describe an impressive range of therapies and beauty treatments. No fewer than eight cubicles have been designed to

'This was the first architectural project that *drew inspiration directly from my sculptures*' «Joseph Caspari»

↑ In the reception area, a white cube of Carrare marble is a good indicator of the luxurious minimalism that awaits the visitor downstairs.

← Architect and sculptor Joseph Caspari, who avoids decorative elements in both his disciplines, realized L'Espace Payot by regarding each element as a monolith from which superfluous elements had to be stripped away.

accommodate various types of massage. Patrons enter one of L'Espace Payot's three hydro-cubicles – made entirely from stone – for water treatments that feature a Vichy shower. Also available is the 'immersion cubicle' and, last but not least, a VIP cubicle in which the prodigiously pampered enjoy the luxury of the entire gamut of therapies and treatments.

Integrating this project into the basement of an existing, relatively old building was an undertaking that Caspari looks back on and calls 'quite complex'. The biggest challenges – what the architect refers to as 'structural inconveniences' – encountered during work on the 1700-m^2 space were solved by lowering the entire floor a full 3 m. This was a significant undertaking, as the existing foundation had to be removed, new beams had to be put into place to support the structure, and a tractor had to be brought in to dig the pool. After eight months, construction was completed.

'This was the first architectural project that drew inspiration directly from my sculptures,' says the architect, who is certain that future projects will follow suit. Caspari likes to view each architectural project for which he is commissioned as a highly magnified extension of his personal, artistic work. 'Both my sculpture and elements designed for my architectural projects are treated as monoliths stripped of all superfluous elements.

In the specific case of L'Espace Payot, the materials I chose are reminiscent of my grey metal sculptures.' Caspari sees little difference between art and architecture. 'I look at architecture and see it as functional sculpture on a much larger scale.'

Following the Parisian luxury project, another hospitality space is in the works; Caspari is currently designing a hotel for a client in Warsaw, Poland. A private villa in Santa Barbara, California, is also on the agenda.

↑ Caspari limited his palette of materials to marble, granite and oak.

↑ In the entire spa, only the
   hammam displays rounded
   shapes.

↖ Having used invisible light
   sources nearly everywhere else in
   the interior, Caspari made a focal
   point of halogen lamps built into
   the floor of the corridor leading
   to the treatment cubicles.

↑ Ancient Roman thermae and classical Turkish baths inspired the architect's concept for the wet areas.

→ To accommodate a modern swimming pool, the entire basement of the 19th-century building had to be lowered by an additional 3 m.

↑ The only illumination in the jacuzzi is provided by underwater lights that create a subterranean, grotto-like ambience.

← The marble bench in the Hammam.

architect
Joseph Caspari
8 rue de Miromesnil
75008 Paris
France
T +33 662 0361 48
F +33 142 6661 48
joseph.caspari@orange.fr

photographer
Antoine Bulot
bulot.ma@voila.fr

legend
01 Wardrobe
02 Waiting area
03 Coaching room
04 Treatment room
05 Pedicure
06 Pool
07 Hammam
08 Vichy shower
09 Beauty room
10 Power plate
11 Fitness
12 Jacuzzi
13 Sauna
14 Showers
15 Retail area
16 Bar
17 Office
18 Hall

Ground floor

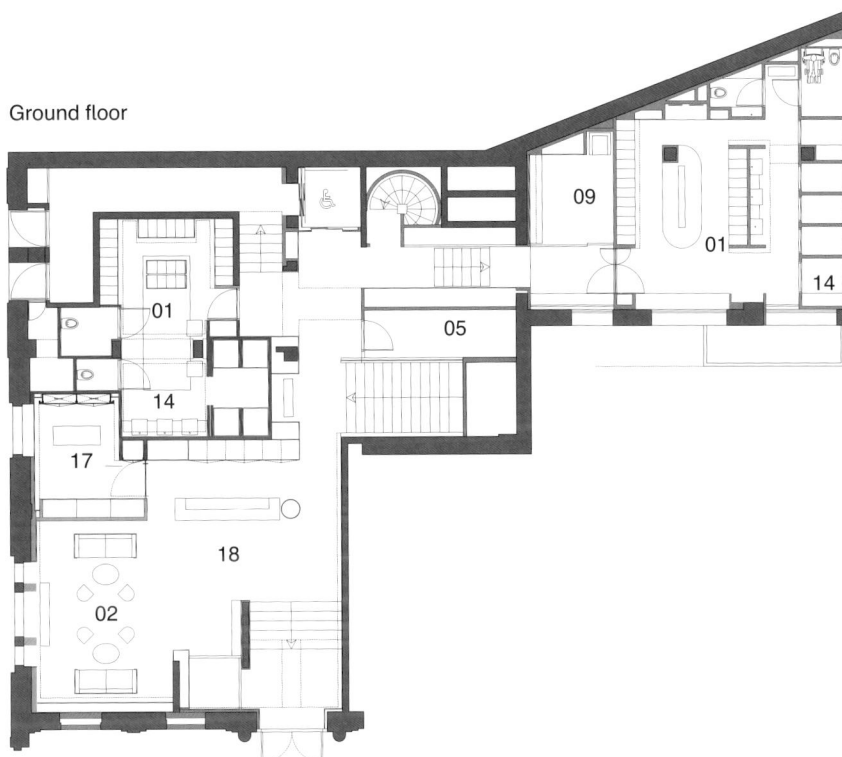

Basement

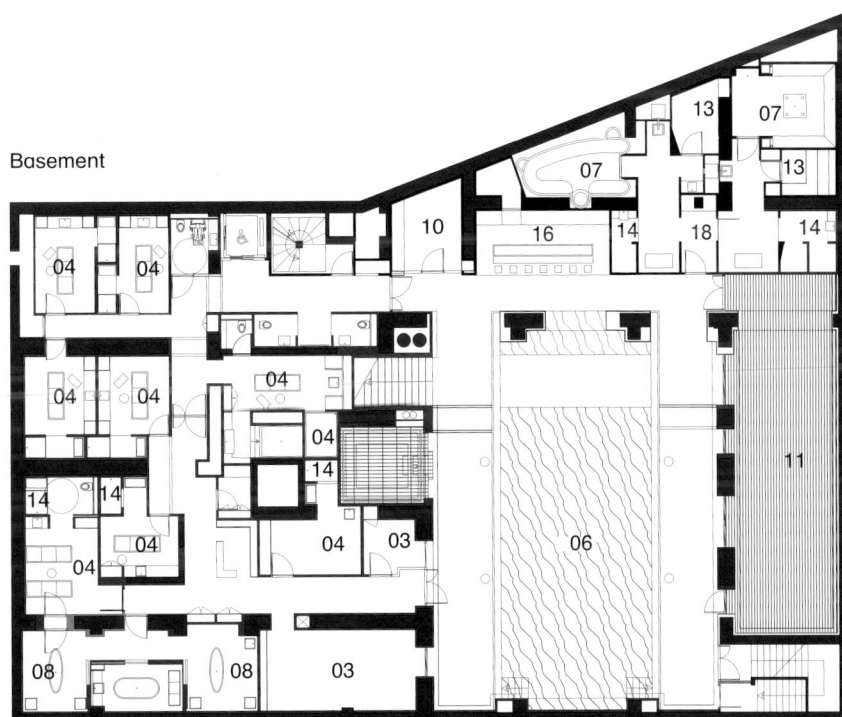

client
John Harris
manufacturer
Kirchberger Tischlerei
lighting design
Christian Ploderer
graphic design
section.d
design.communication

total floor area (m²)
330
duration of construction
8 months
opening
September 2005

project
John Harris Medical Spa
Getreidemarkt 8
1010 Vienna
Austria
T +43 1 907 6979
medicalspa@johnharris.at
www.medspa.at

gps
N 48°12' E 016°22'

BWM Architekten

John Harris Medical Spa

vienna/austria

Text by Stephan Ott

The realms of medicine and wellbeing have often seemed to be mutually exclusive. Many representatives of orthodox medicine define health as the absence of illness, whereas fitness and lifestyle gurus describe illness as a deficiency of wellness. As many in the Asiatic world will tell you, both views fall short of the truth.

In 1983, an American named John Harris opened a fitness centre in Vienna that was to set a new trend for the Western world. Harris believes in a holistic concept that unites health, wellbeing, lifestyle and fitness. The John Harris Medical Spa has medical facilities that offer a variety of checkups, with a doctor in attendance, as well as a range of therapies and treatments, including massage, devoted to wellbeing and beauty. All under the same roof. It was no accident that the planning and realization of the new John Harris Medical Spa was conducted as a holistic enterprise that included several creative disciplines. The entire operation was based on Harris's original concept. According to a spokesman for John Harris, 'The holistic philosophy of the John Harris Medical Spa is supplemented by architecture, design and a treatment plan ingeniously tailored to individual needs.' Vienna-based BWM Architekten handled the planning and building of the medical spa, and a local team known as section.d was responsible for the graphic design. The lighting, which had to satisfy a number of disparate

requirements, is the work of Christian Ploderer. Forming a compact spatial arrangement are the medical diagnostic and therapeutic areas, an exclusive shop and a lounge. Within the various interiors, ordinary materials enjoy new relationships, and light, texture and colour are combined in a fresh and exciting way. The space draws its dynamic air from contrasting elements, such as the juxtaposition of rough natural stone and gleaming golden walls, dark wood and fine ceramics, shiny fabrics and pure white space housing medical equipment. 'The John Harris Medical Spa has an ambitious concept as regards content,' says Erich Bernard of BWM. 'Our architecture mirrors these exigent demands for high quality. Feeling well really does depend on a well-thought-out and harmonious design in terms of space, texture, lighting and colour.' The medical spa has a total surface area of 330 m², divided between ground floor and first floor. The dual-level reception area is the outer interface, where shop, lounge and reception point flow into one another. Gilded walls enclose the area. Used to symbolize the sky, the sun, light

At the John Harris Medical
Spa in Vienna, a double-height
entrance area marks the
spot where shop, lounge
and reception flow together.

and space, gold gives the medical spa a highly distinctive character.

Section.d's graphic design, linked directly to the architecture, is an integral part of the overall impression. The central image of the John Harris corporate identity, or logo, is a red circle, which is repeated throughout the spa, always in combination with figures and forms in lighter shades. All elements of the logo blend discreetly into the surface on which it is featured. 'The idea of the circle symbolizes the fundamental idea behind the new medical spa: to unite mind and body into a harmonious whole,' says Robert Jasensky, managing director of section.d. Lighting, another key design element, has been used as an architectural aid and for presentation purposes, as well as for the more pragmatic function of illuminating the interiors of the complex. Above shimmering slits in the floor, golden walls seem to extend across space. (Light also falls through slits in the ceiling.) Together with reflections from dot-shaped lighting and an occasional wash of light across the surfaces of the interior, the golden wall glistens. In the stairwell, a basin of water bathed in an orange light creates beautiful rippling reflections that fill the space, movements that make a vibrant contrast to the otherwise peaceful mood of the spa. Products displayed in show windows and in the shop and lounge areas stand on large

shining surfaces similar to studio lighting tables. Spots above these surfaces pick out the products and literally 'put them in the spotlight'. A glance through the display window reveals an uncluttered space with a golden aura. Neutral white light brightens the medical and therapeutic areas. Examinations, therapies and treatments are carried out in rooms with gleaming white textile surfaces that feature built-in, dimmable lighting. Illuminated in this way, the space exhales a comfortably relaxed atmosphere that corresponds to the needs of a medical facility. Passers-by see a building with large areas of fenestration that project from the façade – a golden landmark visible from afar. At night, a thin neon strip that runs in a groove around the rusticated exterior walls, signals the close alliance between the medical spa and the neighbouring fitness centre.

↑ The space is surrounded by gleaming, golden walls.

→ Spotlights aimed at products displayed on illuminated surfaces accentuate the merchandise.

John Harris believes in a *holistic concept*,
which unites health, wellbeing, lifestyle
and fitness

↑ Neutral white light
characterizes the medical and
therapeutic areas.

↖ Surfaces clad in soft, shiny
fabrics add a touch of domestic
familiarity to medical checkups,
therapies and treatments.

architect
BWM Architekten
Margaretenplatz 4/L1
1050 Vienna
Austria
T +43 1 205 9070
office@bwm.at
www.bwm.at

photographer
Alexander Koller
office@
alexanderkoller.com
www.alexanderkoller.com
-
Rupert Steiner
office@rupertsteiner.com
www.rupertsteiner.com
-
Bokmeier
claudia.bokmeier@gmx.at

legend
01 Reception
02 Examination room
03 Bar
04 Shop
05 Hall
06 Lavatories

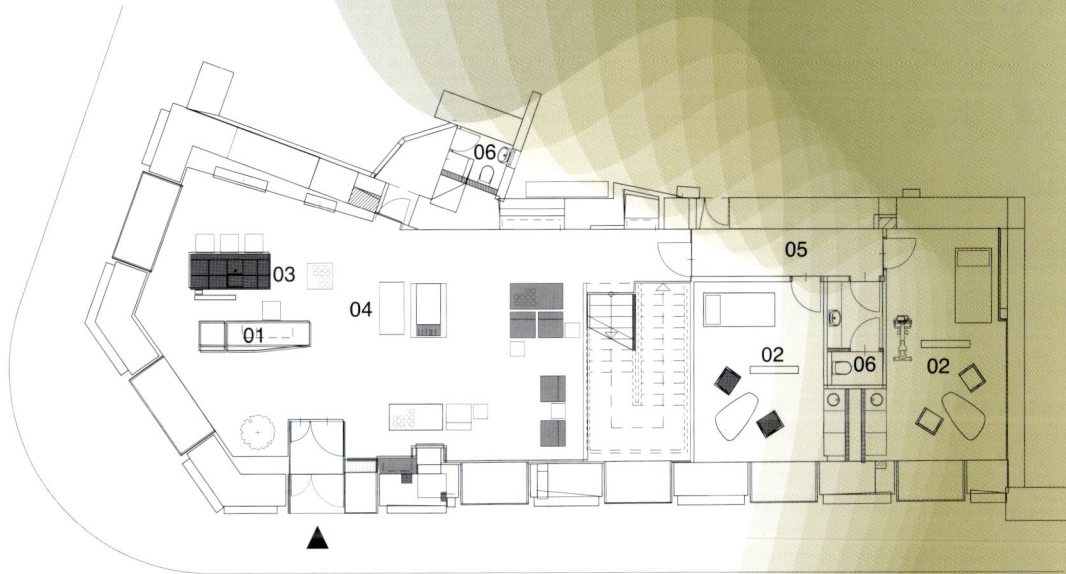

← Graphic design applied directly
   to the architecture is an integral
   part of the overall impression
   conveyed by the interior.

client
Sento Spa and Health Club
structural engineer
Pieters Bouwtechniek
service engineer
Herman de Groot
Projecttechniek
manufacturers
Kloostboer Decor
lighting design
Modular Lighting
Instruments

**mechanical
Installations**
Hellebrekers Techniek
graphic design
Richard Harrington
total floor area (m²)
450
**duration of
construction**
3.5 months
opening
November 2006

project
Sento
Marnixplein 1
1015 ZN Amsterdam
Netherlands
T +31 20 330 1444
F +31 20 627 8484
info@sento.nl
www.sento.nl

gps
N 52°22' E 004°52'

Jeroen van Mechelen

Sento Spa and Health Club

amsterdam/netherlands

Text by Anneke Bokern

Sento Spa and Health Club is an oasis of calm in the midst of Amsterdam's turbulent old town. Sharing a building with a public swimming pool, Sento features fitness, massage and relaxation rooms; a sauna and whirlpool; and a roof terrace with a charming view of the surroundings.

Transparency, quality materials and playful bubble shapes enhance the interior of Sento Spa and Health Club, a centre of fitness and relaxation that rises from a site in Amsterdam formerly occupied by a swimming pool built in 1955. As the only pool serving residents living along the city's canals and in the nearby neighbourhood of Jordaan, the Marnixbad – a complex that included a public bathhouse and laundry, but no proper bar or café – had been an Amsterdam institution before its demolition in 2003.

Subsequently erected on the same spot, the new building consists of three angular volumes: sandwiched between two sections partially clad in brick is a glazed box containing foyer, *grand café* and lounge. The swimming pool is in the largest of the three, which faces south. The volume at the opposite end accommodates Sento Spa and Health Club. The pool is a public facility with a highly

diverse target group, but Sento attracts a more select and rather well-heeled clientele. Membership fees are not for the faint-hearted, interiors are luxurious and prominent Dutch names are among those on the membership list.

The interior designer was Amsterdam architect Jeroen van Mechelen. As a friend of the club's director, Eddie Pasquino, van Mechelen was involved in the project from the start. 'Eddie virtually gave me carte blanche,' says the architect. He had an idea of how the fitness and wellness areas should relate to one another, but otherwise I was free to do more or less as I wished.'

Stepping from the glazed foyer into Sento is like entering another world, an environment noticeably more rounded and more playful than the relatively linear and sparely designed interior of the swimming pool. Then, too, surfaces at Sento demonstrate a higher quality of

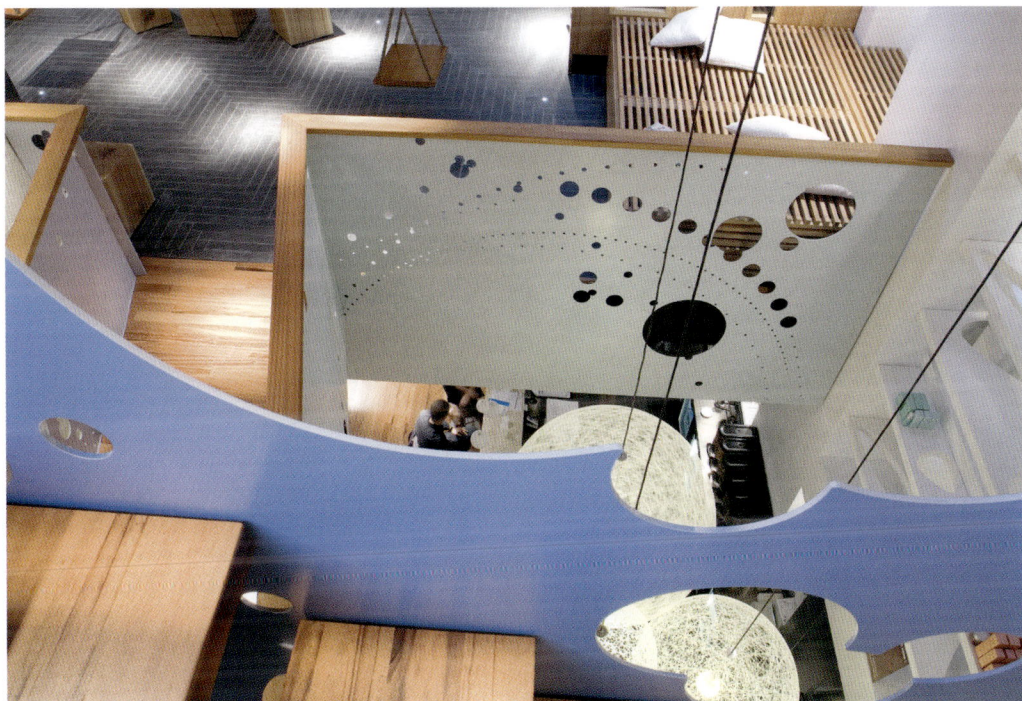

↑ Originally, Sento was going to be called Monkey. The swings are a reference to the earlier name and a popular feature of the club.

← Although Sento has a relatively small floor area (450 m²), a large central void and numerous sightlines give the interior a spacious feel.

Stepping from the glazed foyer into Sento is like *entering another world*

materials. To the right of the entrance, in the reception area, visitors can look up at a void spanned by walkways and crowned by small blobby windows. A leitmotif of bubbles can be found not only in these windows, but also in spherical Random Lights by Moooi, hanging above the reception area, and in the holes that puncture the light blue steel balustrades of the walkways. 'They also harmonize with Sento's logo, which we developed together with the graphic designer,' says van Mechelen. The sense of uncluttered space in a club with a floor area of only 450 m^2 is astonishing. In an attempt to take advantage of everything available to him, the architect made a conscious decision to expand the observer's impression of the interior by creating a feeling of 'openness' wherever possible. Apertures, broad vistas and smaller views dominate a space that has no solid walls obscuring sightlines. Even the treatment cubicles clustered around the reception area have glass walls. Safeguarding the privacy of guests inside these cubicles, however, are curtains that can be drawn as desired. Toilet facilities and lift shaft are freestanding. The latter is lined with travertine slabs. Stressing that the use of natural materials exudes 'an aura of luxury', van Mechelen says the lift and the bubble shapes are the only evidence of 'styling' at Sento. He opted for another natural material in the reception area and the adjoining fitness room, which have parquet flooring. Elsewhere on this floor, visitors find a prevalence of white surfaces, sometimes fitted with LCD monitors. Upstairs, wood panelling has been used on walls, as well as on an undulating ceiling whose

wavy structure is not only decorative but also practical: ductwork and wiring are cleverly concealed behind the attractive overhead surface, made of the same type of wood as the parquet. Next to the stairs, a glazed wall with a sliding door lends access to the club's completely white changing rooms. A protective chain curtain at the entrance is repeated to good effect in the shower curtains. A whirlpool and a sauna occupy the other half of the upper level. A wooden swing suspended from the ceiling on this floor seems somewhat out of place, but, as van Mechelen explains, the club was originally to be called Monkey, which seems to be quite a common name for bathhouses in Japan. Even after the owner chose Sento – a word that means 'bathhouse' in Japanese and 'I feel' in Italian – the swing was still installed and is now a favourite hang-out for most guests.

Continuing up the stairs, the visitor reaches a roof terrace, where van Mechelen has again used wood flooring to create a 'carpet' for various seating arrangements. This, the most urban part of Sento, offers a marvellous view over the roofs of the Jordaan and assures those enjoying the panorama that they are indeed in central Amsterdam. A quick call on the 'butler phone' is rewarded by the arrival of drinks and nibbles. Here in the lap of metropolitan luxury and wellness, all is right with the world.

↑ With the exception of a few cubic 'tree trunk' stools, changing rooms are a minimalist world of white.

→ Random Lights by Moooi and bubble-shaped holes in overhead walkways give the reception-cum-bar a playful atmosphere.

On the first floor, wavy wood panelling covers walls and ceiling, metal chains serve as shower curtains, and basalt flooring completes the picture.

↑ Visitors on the roof terrace have a panoramic view of an Amsterdam neighbourhood known as the Jordaan.

→ The staircase leading to the roof terrace features the same cheerful champagne bubbles that adorn footbridges spanning the void.

architect
Jeroen van Mechelen
Studio JVM
Hamerstraat 3
1021 JT Amsterdam
Netherlands
T +31 20 7889 908
F +31 20 7889 909
studio@studiojvm.nl
www.studiojvm.nl

photographer
Arnout Groen
info@arnoutgroen.com
www.arnoutgroen.com

legend
01 Reception and bar
02 Changing room
03 Floating room
04 Massage room
05 Beauty room
06 Hydro massage room
07 Bridge
08 Relaxation area
09 Wellness room
10 Sauna
11 Scrubstone
12 Whirlpool
13 Fitness room
14 Skylight
15 Mechanical room
16 Showers
17 Lavatories
18 Storage
19 Circulation

Roof terrace

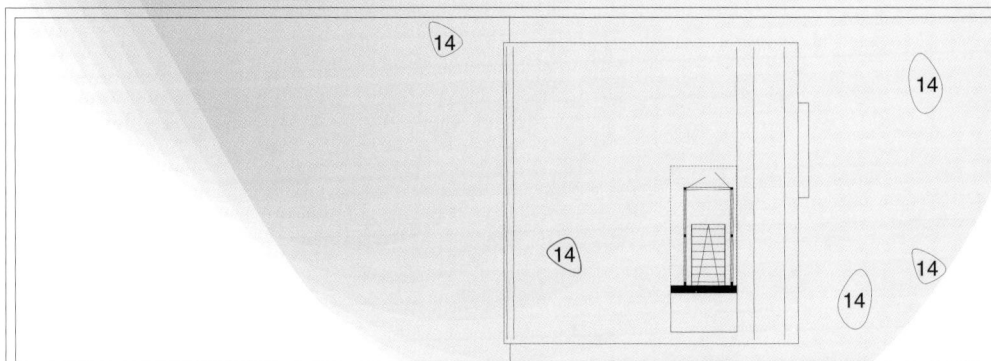

Second floor

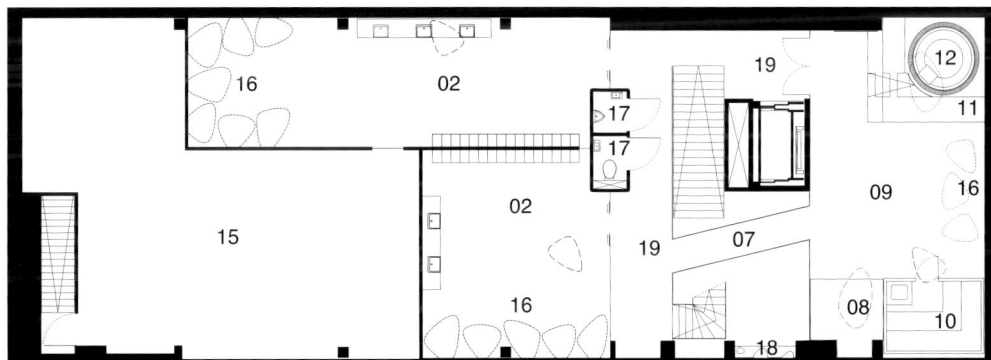

First floor

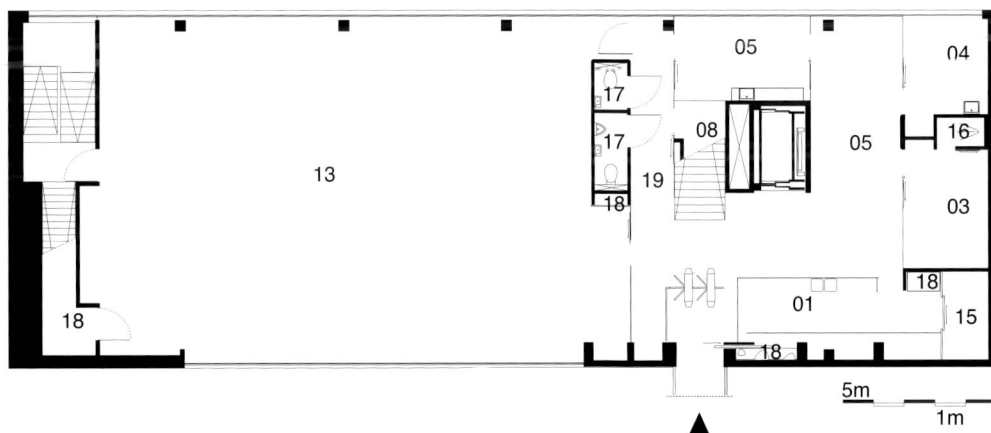

client
ému
engineer
Life House
total floor area (m²)
125
total cost (€)
127,500
budget per m² (€)
1020

duration of construction
1 month
opening
May 2006

project
ému
2F, 8-8-1, Kinuta,
Setagaya-ku
Tokyo 157-0073
Japan
T+81 3 3415 1550
www.emu-emu.jp

gps
N 35°40' E 139°45'

assistant

ému

tokyo/japan

Text by Masaaki Takahashi

Japanese spas often have a dark, enclosed feel, but ému, a stone sauna in Tokyo, bucks the trend with a bright look that reflects the youthful approach of its designers. By fusing meticulously created visual devices with contemporary tastes, they gave this bijou sauna a highly distinctive character.

At around 40°C, stone saunas offer a milder temperature than conventional saunas and place less strain on the body. Coupled with Japan's recent vogue for detox treatments, this fact has only added to their popularity. Relaxation-seeking clients lie on heated slabs of bedrock, soothed by the far-infrared radiation emanating from natural minerals and gently warmed to induce slight perspiration. The rapid growth of this niche industry is also due to the ease of setting up such facilities and to minimal start-up costs: these saunas can be low-key affairs consisting simply of stone slabs arranged throughout the space in question. Stone saunas are typified by muted lighting and soft colour schemes, and Japanese- or Oriental-themed interiors are prevalent. Looking to create a highly polished interior for an exclusively female clientele, however, the owner of ému, a sauna in Tokyo, invited Assistant – a young outfit consisting of Megumi Matsubara, Hiroi Ariyama and Motohiro Sunouchi – to come up with something slightly different. Advocates of interdisciplinary design, the three often enter into joint ventures with both individuals and groups. Active at home and abroad, they boast a wide-ranging portfolio filled with graphic-design and interior projects encompassing both analogue and digital solutions.

The group is fast becoming a hot new name in the design world. At ému, rather than the dim, enclosed interior often found in a conventional Japanese spa, the first image Assistant came up with was a meadow overlooking the sea. Matsubara observes that during the research stage they saw the majority of sauna facilities going for a darkened, Asian-style décor and so were tempted to try something new. 'We wanted to create a place where visitors could feel as though they were at a resort, lying on the grass next to the seashore.' This idea was expressed through architectural design that took white as its keynote colour, contrasting it with bright greens and yellows in sweet-wrapper hues. To this was added an open feel generated by a wood-decked balcony. Expecting a more stereotypical, sombre ambience, the client at first put up some resistance to the design, but was brought round in the end.

ému can be found on the first floor of an apartment block in Tokyo's residential Setagaya district. To the left of the entrance lies a wood deck that acts as both a waiting area and a place to cool down after the sauna. The glass façade gives visitors the agreeable feeling of being able to cast an eye across the entire reception area. Visitors usually take off their shoes upon entering spas in Japan, and

↑ Carpet gradually merges with white mosaic tiles featuring a striking floral motif. Tiles curling up from the floor form the cladding of a reception counter.

← Acrylic-resin partitions are adorned with lines, white droplets and, at the bottom, a plant motif that differs with each panel.

the designers have used this custom to their advantage by integrating changes in texture in the floor which are meant to alter the visitor's mood and to heighten anticipation. Stepping inside, she enjoys the sensation of plush carpeting underfoot, followed by the feeling of smooth, cool tiles extending from the reception desk. According to Matsubara, this interior is similar in some ways to that of a sento (Japanese for 'bathhouse'), where visitors remove their shoes at the entrance before making their way to the baths. The floors and walls of a sento are usually covered in white tiles, giving the space a clean, airy atmosphere instantly recognizable to Japanese guests; this was the reason behind the choice of tiles for ému. In a rather tongue-in-cheek way, the designers went on to point out that, despite its resemblance to a sento, ému is somewhat different. Their poppy mosaic and cute waiting room, reminiscent of an aviary, are fitting touches for a sauna reserved for the fair sex.

Stepping inside the stone sauna itself, the guest is enveloped in a pale mist. Here, silhouettes of plants and droplets of differing sizes are etched onto the translucent partitions that separate the stone slabs. Printed onto shatterproof film with a special, Israeli-made ink-jet printer capable of reproducing images in white ink, the pattern was then affixed to the acrylic-resin panels. 'Thanks to the importer's advice, we discovered the most effective way to use the printer and were able to demonstrate its capabilities really well,' comments Ariyama. The designers created overall harmony in this part of the spa by blending the swirling mist with blue spatters on the tiled walls and white droplets printed on the panels. Each partition features a different type of plant positioned near its base and visible to the woman relaxing on the heated slab. ému offers 60- and 90-minutes sessions in the sauna, which can be topped off with a massage.

'We wanted to create a place where visitors could feel as though they were at a resort, lying on the grass next to the *seashore*'

«Megumi Matsubara of Assistant»

↑ The palette of pale colors used at ému is uncommon in Japan, where the owners of most relaxation facilities prefer darker tones.

→ The bright green waiting area contrasts with the white walls.

A wood-decked area reminiscent of those at seaside resorts invites patrons to cool down after leaving the sauna.

architect
assistant
4-28-8-606, Yoyogi,
Shibuya-ku
Tokyo 151-0053
Japan
T +81 3 5809 0903
tokyo@withassistant.net
www.withassistant.net

photographer
Motohiro Sunouchi
www.withassistant.net

legend
01 Reception
02 Waiting room
03 Changing room
04 Stone spa
05 Cool-down room
06 Massage room
07 Shower
08 Lavatories
09 Staff room
10 Wood deck

1000   3000

← The pattern on the partitions
– which has also been described
as 'a waterfall' – reinforces the
sense of a natural environment.

client
Yi-Spa-Studio/Marco Thiele
and Stephan Gustavus
manufacturers
Christian Steller, Udo
Theiss, Saier Electric and
Bernd Schreiner
graphic design
XIX Gesellschaft für
x-beliebige Werbung

total floor area (m²)
120
**duration of
construction**
6 months
opening
May 2006

project
Yi-Spa-Studio
Monbijouplatz 3
10178 Berlin
Germany
T +49 30 2887 9665
F +49 30 2887 9660
relax@yi-spa.com
www.yi-spa.com

gps
N 52°31' E 013°23'

plajer & franz studio

Yi-Spa-Studio

berlin/germany

Text by Anneke Bokern

Relaxation is high on the agenda at Europe's first Yi-Spa-Studio. The interior that plajer & franz designed for Yi-Spa combines cool Asian minimalism, a warm sense of wellness and dark colours. An unusual Thai massage studio in Chiang Mai served as a model for the design but the final concept is a cosmopolitan city-spa-studio.

The Yi-Spa-Studio in central Berlin is the first of its kind in Europe. 'In Thailand, where the concept originated, there are studios like this on every street corner,' says Alexander Plajer of plajer & franz, the outfit responsible for the interior design. 'We've been involved in projects in Thailand over the years, so we've been frequent visitors to the country, where we like going to spas to chill out.' Massage is at the heart of Yi-Spa's programme. 'It's not a case of simply pummelling the client. There's much more to it. First tea is brought in, along with some dried fruit. Then your feet are washed and massaged. Only then does the body massage begin.' It's a comprehensive programme that promotes wellbeing, and interior design contributes to the overall ambience.

'Marco Thiele and Stephan Gustavus, who commissioned the spa, run a communications agency, but they wanted to diversify,' Plajer explains. 'They've been good friends of us for the past 12 years, and we've worked with them often, there is a good synergy between us.' It was obvious from the start that the spaces would be influenced by cool Asian minimalism, while also radiating a sense of warmth. In search of inspiration, Plajer made yet another trip to Thailand before working on his designs. 'Each day I'd visit another studio in Bangkok and take a good look around.'

The design centres on individualism. 'Many Thai studios are very beautiful, but they can seem interchangeable. We think authenticity is extremely important. When we are in Batavia, we would rather tuck into a good dish of roast pork than some kind of "world food". We think authenticity is a general trend at the moment.' plajer & franz's design was inspired by a massage studio in Chiang Mai. 'You go to an island in the middle of a river, where you're massaged beneath tall trees, but you still have a clear view of the sky. You cross the river on stepping stones to reach the massage couches. It is breathtakingly beautiful and bursting with character,' Plajer enthuses. With this image in mind, the designers distilled a modular

↑ At the Yi-Spa-Studio, even the towels are works of sculpture. Before the massage treatment starts, the guest is invited to set the lighting in the room at the desired intensity.

← A mosaic in mother-of-pearl covers the surface of the reception counter.

we know the way to 7th heaven

concept of the space for use in Berlin, where floors in each of the studio's three massage areas are covered in pebbles and inset with slabs of slate or marble. 'It's extremely cost effective. You can lay this kind of flooring anywhere, no matter what the basic floor is like.' The paving stones lead to an area of 'wellness', which is demarcated by the cuff-like strip of wood that encompasses it. Like a broad ribbon, the strip lines the edges of floors, walls and ceiling, even delineating a washstand. A scattering of round, differently sized openings in wall and ceiling strips function for the most part as light sources. Behind one circles, however, is a stylized hourglass, and directly above the head of the client lying on the massage couch is a monitor displaying a series of relaxing images of blue skies and fleecy clouds. Gentle background music enhances the sense of serenity. Clients can dim the lights at will. 'Everything had to be very stylish,' says designer Werner Franz. Above all, he adds, no Asiatic or esoteric kitsch. The claim of yi 'we know the way to seventh heaven' can be sensed in every aspect of the design.

Materials and colours are natural and warm. Shapes are simple. Each massage room features a unique colour concept based on a single shade: aubergine, charcoal and white. In the white room, a magenta logo on a glass partition steals the show. Wood – used to make both 'cuff' and purpose-designed furniture – has been stained to match the colour of each room. Yi-Spa's logo, a large print of an Asian flower, looks resplendent on the curtains. The reception counter in the lobby is imported. A mosaic in mother-of-pearl covers its entire surface. 'When we designed the place, Thiele showed us a small piece of mother-of-pearl mosaic which we used as a table top,' says Franz. It is suspended above a block of slate into which a small tree has been inserted. The floor of the lobby is paved in dark stone, and dark colours warm the walls. Here, too, highlights are provided by glass in magenta, the studio's trademark colour.

Yi-Spa-Studio opened in May 2006. 'The interior was actually ready in February, but the masseurs still had to be trained. They often used us as guinea pigs. That, of course, was wonderful,' says Franz with a laugh. He is now a regular customer of the studio he designed.

It was obvious from the start that the spaces would be influenced by *cool Asian minimalism* while radiating a sense of warmth

↑ In the white massage room, a magenta Yi-Spa-Studio logo contrasts with the whiteness of walls and pebbles and the warmth of the wooden strip.

→ What looks like another round display in the wooden wall is, in fact, a stylized magenta clock.

Chocolaty, feel-good cosiness blend astonishingly well with Asian minimalism in the darkest of the massage rooms.

client
Confidential
manufacturers
Tanseisha, Nakahara
house kogei and Tsuruya
Shouten
lighting consultant
Spangle
graphic design
DRAFT

total floor area (m²)
89.7
capacity
8 clients
duration of construction
2 months
opening
October 2006

project
Caon Toyosu
2-4-9-2F Lalaport Toyosu
Kotoku, Tokyo 135-8614
Japan
T +81 3 6910 1315
info@caon.jp
www.caon.jp

gps
N 35°40' E 139°45'

TONERICO:INC.
Caon Toyosu
tokyo/japan

Text by Masaaki Takahashi

A water-themed design and warm, natural materials – surfaces of wood and stone on all sides – highlight the interior of this aromatherapy and reflexology salon, a place that soothes the soul and exudes an aura of luxury very rarely found in large-scale commercial complexes.

Over the last ten years or so in Japan, aromatherapy and reflexology have started to penetrate public awareness. The opposite is true in the UK, and it is the practice of aromatherapy and reflexology in that country which has strongly influenced the design of Japanese spas providing these treatments. The interiors of such facilities tend to incorporate predominantly Western or typically English motifs. One example is Caon's original Ginza salon, which has the ambience of a spa provided for guests at a high-class British hotel. To differentiate between it and the new Toyosu branch, the owners switched their focus to a Japanese-style interior. The new direction taken is also evident in the salon's meticulous service. The company behind Caon operates a wide range of aromatherapy and reflexology facilities: not only fashionable 'healing' salons and spas, but also a technical school at which students learn to become professional practitioners. The firm also maintains its own organic herb gardens.

The client, deeply impressed by Tonerico's design for a confectionery shop specializing in Japanese sweets called *wagashi*, hoped to tap into a similarly Japanese aesthetic in his own project. He subsequently invited Tonerico, a Tokyo-based design collective known for its sophisticated contemporary work, to plan and realize the interior of Caon's Toyosu branch.

Tonerico chose water as a theme for the design. The reason lies in Caon's location: the second floor of a large-scale shopping mall, Lalaport Toyosu, a development that occupies a former industrial zone on a reclaimed section of Tokyo's waterfront. Formerly home to factories and thermal power plants, the district remains strongly associated with the concept of the sea. Situated a stone's throw from the classy shopping area of Ginza, Toyosu is undergoing major redevelopment, which includes huge building projects like Lalaport and neighbouring condominiums.

On the right as you walk through the entranceway stands a basin chiselled from a block of limestone, a material quarried on the shores of Okinawa. Water wells up and flows down its sides in a never-ending cycle. 'Water not only adds a touch of serenity to a space, but simultaneously adds movement, making it an element that powerfully appeals to the emotions,' says Ken Kimizuka of Tonerico.

From the entrance, visitors step into a narrow corridor that gradually pulls them away from reality and eases awareness of the shopping complex just outside. 'It's the same sort of sensation experienced when making your way to your seat for a tea ceremony,' says Kimizuka. Inside, benches and stools of solid wood are pleasant to

SMILE AND THE WHOLE WORLD WILL SMILE WITH YOU, GIVE AND IT WILL RETURN TO YOU.

architect
plajer & franz studio
Erkelenzdamm 59-61
10999 Berlin
Germany
T +49 30 6165 580
F +49 30 6165 5819
studio@plajer-franz.de
www.plajer-franz.de

photographers
diephotodesigner.de
contact@diephotodesigner.de
www.diephotodesigner.de
-
XIX Gesellschaft für
x-beliebige Werbung
mot@xix-berlin.de
www.xix-berlin.de

legend
01 Lobby
02 Treatment room
03 Lavatories
04 Staff area

1 m

↖ A wooden strip with integrated
seating, sinks and displays
embraces the interior like a cuff,
forming the leitmotif of Yi-Spa-
Studio.

← Above the couch, a round display
offers a glimpse of a picture-
perfect digital sky.

← Asian imagery but no oriental
kitsch at the Yi-Spa-Studio.

client
Confidential
manufacturers
Tanseisha, Nakahara
house kogei and Tsuruya
Shouten
lighting consultant
Spangle
graphic design
DRAFT

total floor area (m²)
89.7
capacity
8 clients
**duration of
construction**
2 months
opening
October 2006

project
Caon Toyosu
2-4-9-2F Lalaport Toyosu
Kotoku, Tokyo 135-8614
Japan
T +81 3 6910 1315
info@caon.jp
www.caon.jp

gps
N 35°40' E 139°45'

TONERICO:INC.
Caon Toyosu
tokyo/japan

Text by Masaaki Takahashi

A water-themed design and warm, natural materials – surfaces of wood and stone on all sides – highlight the interior of this aromatherapy and reflexology salon, a place that soothes the soul and exudes an aura of luxury very rarely found in large-scale commercial complexes.

Over the last ten years or so in Japan, aromatherapy and reflexology have started to penetrate public awareness. The opposite is true in the UK, and it is the practice of aromatherapy and reflexology in that country which has strongly influenced the design of Japanese spas providing these treatments. The interiors of such facilities tend to incorporate predominantly Western or typically English motifs. One example is Caon's original Ginza salon, which has the ambience of a spa provided for guests at a high-class British hotel. To differentiate between it and the new Toyosu branch, the owners switched their focus to a Japanese-style interior. The new direction taken is also evident in the salon's meticulous service. The company behind Caon operates a wide range of aromatherapy and reflexology facilities: not only fashionable 'healing' salons and spas, but also a technical school at which students learn to become professional practitioners. The firm also maintains its own organic herb gardens.

The client, deeply impressed by Tonerico's design for a confectionery shop specializing in Japanese sweets called *wagashi*, hoped to tap into a similarly Japanese aesthetic in his own project. He subsequently invited Tonerico, a Tokyo-based design collective known for its sophisticated contemporary work, to plan and realize the interior of Caon's Toyosu branch.

Tonerico chose water as a theme for the design. The reason lies in Caon's location: the second floor of a large-scale shopping mall, Lalaport Toyosu, a development that occupies a former industrial zone on a reclaimed section of Tokyo's waterfront. Formerly home to factories and thermal power plants, the district remains strongly associated with the concept of the sea. Situated a stone's throw from the classy shopping area of Ginza, Toyosu is undergoing major redevelopment, which includes huge building projects like Lalaport and neighbouring condominiums.

On the right as you walk through the entranceway stands a basin chiselled from a block of limestone, a material quarried on the shores of Okinawa. Water wells up and flows down its sides in a never-ending cycle. 'Water not only adds a touch of serenity to a space, but simultaneously adds movement, making it an element that powerfully appeals to the emotions,' says Ken Kimizuka of Tonerico.

From the entrance, visitors step into a narrow corridor that gradually pulls them away from reality and eases awareness of the shopping complex just outside. 'It's the same sort of sensation experienced when making your way to your seat for a tea ceremony,' says Kimizuka. Inside, benches and stools of solid wood are pleasant to

The custom-made washbasin on
the right is made of Okinawan
limestone.

the touch. Paulownia-wood flooring in the treatment area has a particularly soft, warm feel. In Japan, Paulownia is an expensive, high-quality material often used in traditional furniture such as chests and boxes for holding keepsakes and other precious items. For this reason, many Japanese people find its texture immensely soothing. Although slippers are usually worn in the treatment rooms, the wood retains enough warmth to make going barefoot a comfortable option. Despite the delicate nature of Paulownia and the high degree of maintenance it requires, designers took the bold step of installing it as flooring, thus taking advantage of its distinctive warmth. In the unlikely setting of a mall, their aim was to produce an aura of elegance you'd be more likely to expect from a luxury hotel, and Caon Toyosu's guests seem extremely satisfied with the result.

With three treatment rooms, five reflexology chairs, a backyard and a waiting area to squeeze into the small, single-level premises, the designers were forced to make competent use of every spare centimetre. Mirrors dotted about the facility help to make rooms feel larger, while the 4-m-high ceiling was also used to good effect. Painted a dark grey, it melts away, high above the indirect lighting placed near floor level in each room. Dimmer switches installed under the therapists' chairs allow for the effortless adjustment of illumination. Sensory deprivation is vital in making any space into a setting for relaxation, and Tonerico's designers needed to tone down stimuli affecting the five senses. 'One of the points you have to bear in mind when designing relaxation facilities,' says Kimizuka, 'is how to control each of the senses.' All elements in this interior – from subdued lighting, natural materials and delightful textures to soft tones, translucent fabrics and the semi-frosted glass used in the façade – are evidence of the designers' judicious control of this Japanese-tinged environment.

'One of the points you have to bear in mind when designing relaxation facilities is how to control *each of the senses*'
«Ken Kimizuka»

Visitors to Caon enjoy walking
on the Paulownia-wood flooring,
which is pleasant to the touch.
Semi-frosted glass blurs the view.

Lighting levels vary in each room, and the palette of materials is limited. It was the designer's intention to sharpen the guest's senses – especially touch and smell – as she moves deeper into the space.

↑ Thanks to indirect lighting, the 4-m-high ceiling, painted grey, seems to fade away. Dimmer switches operated by the therapist alter the intensity of light in the room.

→ Flooring of burnt Paulownia wood and a wall featuring paint mixed with glass beads are in contrast with the more natural materials used at the Caon salon.

→ The reflexology room is dark and calm, making visitors forget that they are in a big shopping mall.

architect
TONERICO:INC.
6-18-2-902 Jingumae
Shibuya
Tokyo 150-0001
Japan
T +81 3 5468 0608
F +81 3 5468 0609
tonerico.inc@nifty.com
www.tonerico-inc.com

photographer
Nacása & Partners Inc.
Atsushi Nakamichi
pressrelation@nacasa.co.jp
www.nacasa.co.jp/index.html

legend
01 Reception
02 Cashier
03 Changing room
04 Reflexology room
05 Body-treatment room
06 Staff room

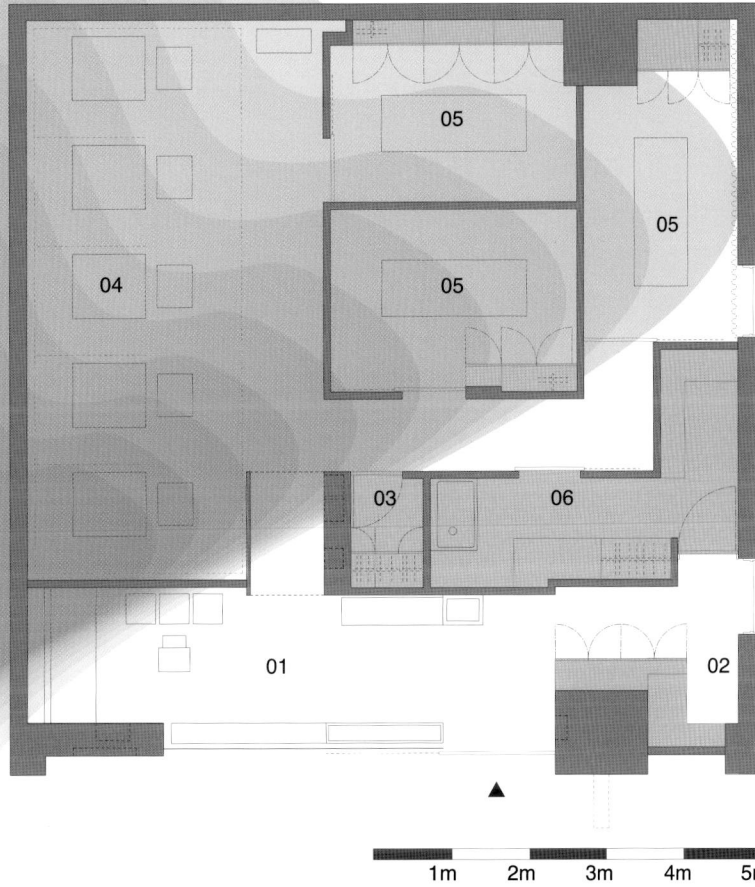

1m 2m 3m 4m 5m

client
Municipality of Algyõ
lead designers
Jenõ Kapy and István Murka
mechanical engineer
Attila Braun
total floor area (m²)
2000

gps
N 46°20' E 020°12'

Dóm Architecture Studio

Thermal Baths

algyõ/hungary

Text by Joeri Bruyninckx

In January 2005, Dóm Architecture Studio of Budapest presented its competition entry for a complex featuring several thermal baths to be built in Algyõ, Hungary. The very traditional design ultimately selected by the jury, however, had almost nothing in common with the proposal submitted by architects Jenõ Kapy and Istvan Murka.

The designers at Dóm Architecture Studio were convinced that the right architectural environment could inject a note of harmony into the municipality's brief for a complex to be built in Algyõ, Hungary: participants in the design competition for this project were to consider two target groups – those with an interest in sport and those seeking a wellness venue – and to submit a plan that could be realized in several phases. Shunning 'the trend of loud, noisy and over-stimulating public-bathing complexes, à la amusements parks', Dóm's designers set out 'to create something holistic and meditative'. Their basic guidelines were pure and simple: a well-considered use of natural materials, a seamless space with smooth transitions, and a plan that could be realized on a limited budget. What appears to make their project unique is that they applied these guidelines on several highly diverse conceptual levels – past and present, landscape and architecture, inside and outside – and on all levels the materials used do indeed blend in one seamless flow. The local jury, however, was less enthusiastic about the concept, ultimately opting for a far more common design.

The architects reintroduced several striking local elements into the exterior architecture of the complex. The building site was formerly an industrial zone occupied by factory buildings serving the oil industry, and the characteristic pitched roofs and elongated buildings in Dóm Architecture's proposal were intended to strike a familiar chord with the residents of Algyõ. Furthermore, the plan indicates the use of a local and typically Hungarian locust wood as the visible finish of all surfaces – either exposing

↑ Daylight is drawn into the central arcade by means of small, strategically positioned patios and apertures in the roof, which together create a sense of openness.

← Ceiling heights vary from 12 m above the large exercise pool to 8 m above the much smaller plunge bath.

the light structure or hiding the subterrainian reinforced concrete structure – without exception: exterior and interior walls, partitions, floors and ceilings. Yes, the seamlessness they were aiming for is conceptual – inexpensive, natural materials used in a rural environment – but it is also an experiential facet of the design. Wooden walls and ceilings are interrupted only at strategic spots by large transparent windows and smaller openings to admit light. The idea is to provide the complex with both direct and indirect light, thus creating an open atmosphere. And the use of narrow, geometric apertures as a source of light gives the architecture a very contemporary look. These 'light slots' balance out the more traditional elements of the design, as well as the naturalness with which the complex becomes one with the landscape.

The ground plan of the complex is composed of three parallel zones, each with a clearly delineated function. The main building section – which accommodates entrance area, lockers and changing rooms, among other things – has been placed as close to the street as possible 'to allow for expansion during the second and later phases'. This volume lends access to a second zone: a central arcade. The use of an arcade as the central element is a reference to the classic layout of the traditional Turkish baths that were once so popular in this area, owing to the former occupation of this region by the Turks. The 8-m-high portico offers room for reclining chairs and fitness equipment and connects the various interiors of the third zone with one another. The third and final zone contains separate areas for a large exercise pool, a sauna, a plunge bath and a lounging pool, which is linked to an outdoor pool and a large sun terrace.

To draw a sufficient amount of light into the central zone of the complex, with its high roof ridges, Dóm Architecture placed small patios between the various zones. Bordered by glass walls, these intermediate islands of green contribute greatly to the smooth transition between indoors and outdoors. In due time, several theme gardens would have been added to the sun terrace as well. Above all else, the final result was meant to be an oasis that would 'initiate the process of healing by creating an environment of natural harmony and peacefulness'.

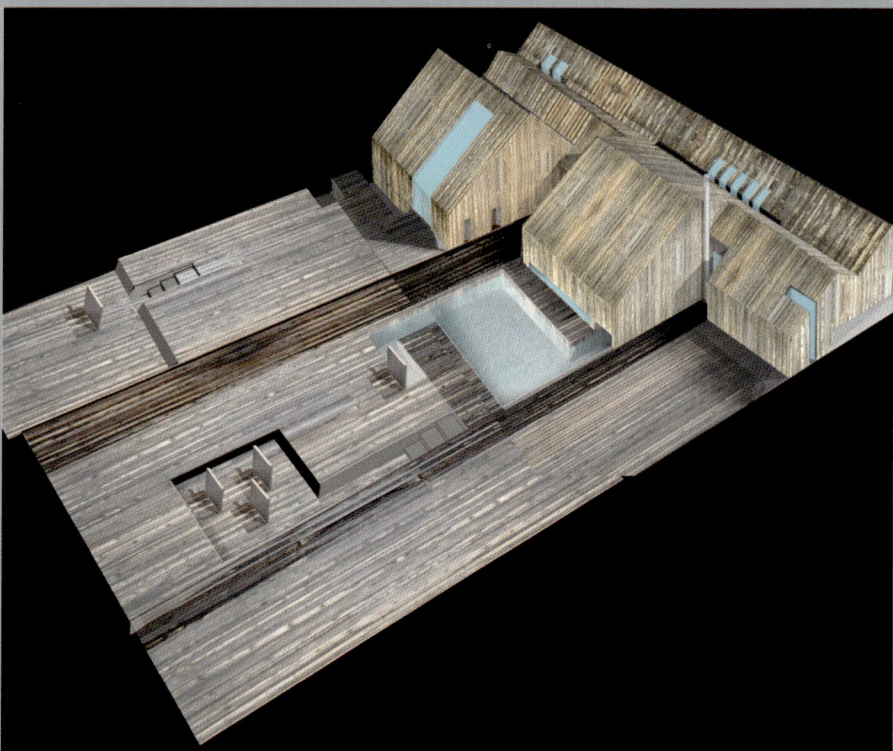

The designers shunned 'the trend of loud, noisy and over-stimulating public-bathing complexes, à la amusements parks' in their efforts 'to create something *holistic and meditative*'

architect
Dóm Architecture Studio
Régiposta u. 5. V/2
1052 Budapest
T +36 1 235 0814
F +36 1 235 0815
dom@dom.hu
www.dom.hu

legend

01 Lounge area
02 Wardrobe
03 Cashier
04 Lockers
05 Bathing deck
06 Cold water immersion basin
07 Indoor lounging basin
08 Training basin
09 Sauna
10 Showers
11 Lavatories
12 Office
13 Storage
14 Service room
15 Circulation

Ground floor

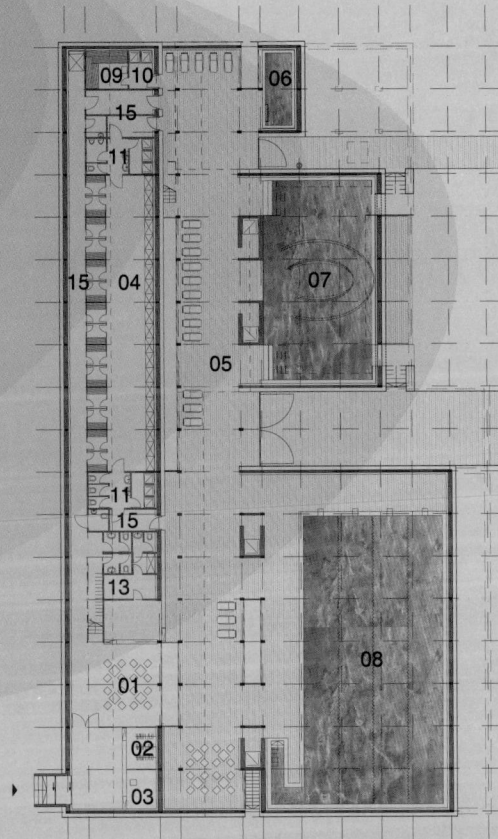

Gallery level

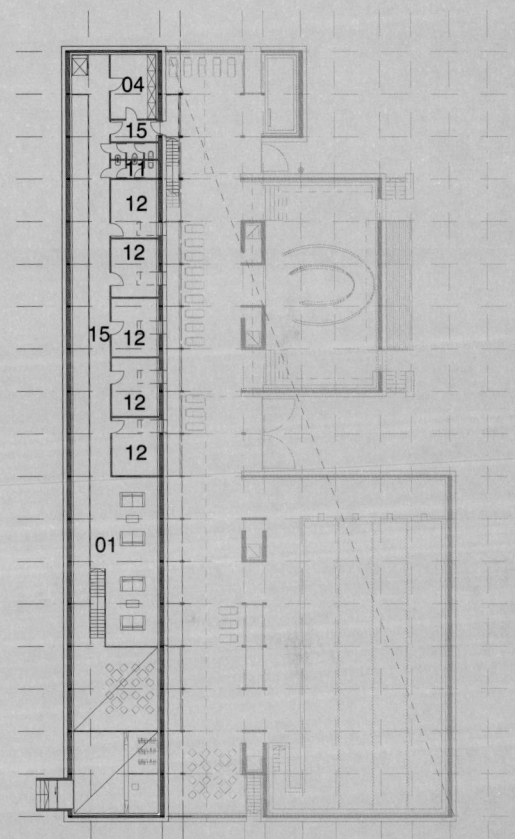

↖ The plan shows a complex that is as close to the street as possible. The main building, which faces the street, accommodates entrance hall, changing rooms and offices.

↖ The complex is designed to be experienced as a seamless combination of glass and wood. Beneath the uniform cladding of Hungarian locust wood, however, the volumes are supported by reinforced-concrete structures covered in weatherproof metal panelling.

← A sun terrace behind the bathhouses was intended to be completed at a later date. Positioned slightly above the rest of the landscape, the terrace would have been supplemented with various thematic gardens.

Section 02
Salons

Text by Karim Rashid

'Don't go changing, to try and please me ...don't change the color of your hair'
Billy Joel, 1976

It is so great to see that in the built environment we are not aesthetically bankrupt. I am always amazed when I meet someone whom I do not think is physically attractive at first sight and, by getting to know that person, they become more and more beautiful to me. I see their features as a complex relationship of mannerisms, cognitive and spiritual, and the physiological connectivity of the senses. Beauty is epitomized through the combinatory arrangement of all these factors; hence beauty is more than surface, more than skin. It is a deeper inseparable relationship between the inner and the outer, an osmosis of aesthetics. Therefore beauty is not a question of taste, of personal likes and dislikes, but a learned appreciation, an experimental process. This underlying depth of beauty means that content plays a primary role in the beauty of things. Paintings, objects, art, architecture and space all manifest their aesthetics through content. When the visual and the concept are inseparable, we have beauty. Something beautiful has content. I call this holistic design.

In several of the salon interiors featured here, we see a movement towards defining the space for beautification as a very scientific or almost medical approach. We have embraced the idea that technology and science can make us more beautiful. From plastic surgery to laser eye surgery, medical shifts act as a platform to inspire designers to create salons that are no longer 'salons' but places of beautification. I see these spaces as de-stressers that bring enjoyment, not encumbrances, and that simplify tasks, thus increasing our levels of engagement and of beauty. At the same time, I believe we need outrageous proposals – radical ideas – to counter the world and the things we live with. To challenge the creative process, I endorse the type of heresy that will spawn a multitude of values, beliefs, styles and ideologies and will allow them to coexist in our new interior landscapes. Fortunately, there is no one school or language, but it is evident here that we celebrate the new, that change is a cultural need, and that we are really alive in a contemporary world.

'Pleasure is more psychological than physical. Health is more physical than psychological. *Beauty is both*'

«Karim»

client
Dermalogica
engineers
Mirahmadi and Associates
and Sigma Design
Structural Engineers
manufacturer
Millwork

total floor area (m²)
155.5
**duration of
construction**
5 months
opening
January 2004

project
Dermalogica on Montana
1022 Montana Avenue
Santa Monica, CA 90403
USA
T +1 310 260 8682
www.dermalogicaon
montana.com

gps
N 34°1' E -118°29'

Abramson Teiger Architects

Dermalogica on Montana

santa monica/usa

Text by Tim Groen

Referencing the plastic nature of human skin, Abramson Teiger Architects designed a skin-treatment centre in Santa Monica for Dermalogica. Because the public associates Dermalogica with a line of beauty products, it was as important to showcase the merchandise as it was to create an inviting and unique facility.

'The client didn't want a typical "spa look", and we didn't either,' recalls Trevor Abramson of Abramson Teiger Architects. Besides a desire for something out of the ordinary and for what Abramson describes as 'your basic programmatic requirements', the client, skin-care brand Dermalogica, did not have a long list of specific demands. All Dermalogica envisioned was a flagship store – its first – that would prominently feature the product line, while functioning as a skin-care treatment centre. The result is Dermalogica on Montana, a name that combines the brand with the exact location of the Santa Monica facility. The architects, whose practice is based in Culver City, California, quickly developed the basis for their concept and, during the first brainstorming sessions, presented an initial model that was 'cut and pasted and held together with tape'. It was then that Abramson and his partner, Douglas Teiger, came up with the key components of the

project. With an eye to creating a serene and soothing atmosphere, they opted to employ as much white as possible. Abramson also stresses that white was chosen to emphasize Dermalogica's colour-coded packaging. The product comes first, according to Abramson, who felt it was important to create displays that would fit seamlessly into the overall setting, keeping the idea of items for sale at a low pitch rather than making sales an all too obvious objective.

The focus of the space, therefore, is a trio of freestanding 'pods' in which skin treatments take place. Both Dermalogica and the architects were determined to avoid the corridor-with-rooms-in-the-back model, which dominates the bulk of contemporary skin and beauty centres. The idea of organically shaped pods made a distinct departure from conventional facilities of this sort. And an unconventional image is exactly what this client

↑ Product displays are key elements of the interior design. The wall in the background is clad in rough concrete tiles.

← The large window, a modernist element of the original 1920s Spanish-Colonial façade, slides open in the daytime to make the most of Southern California's climate.

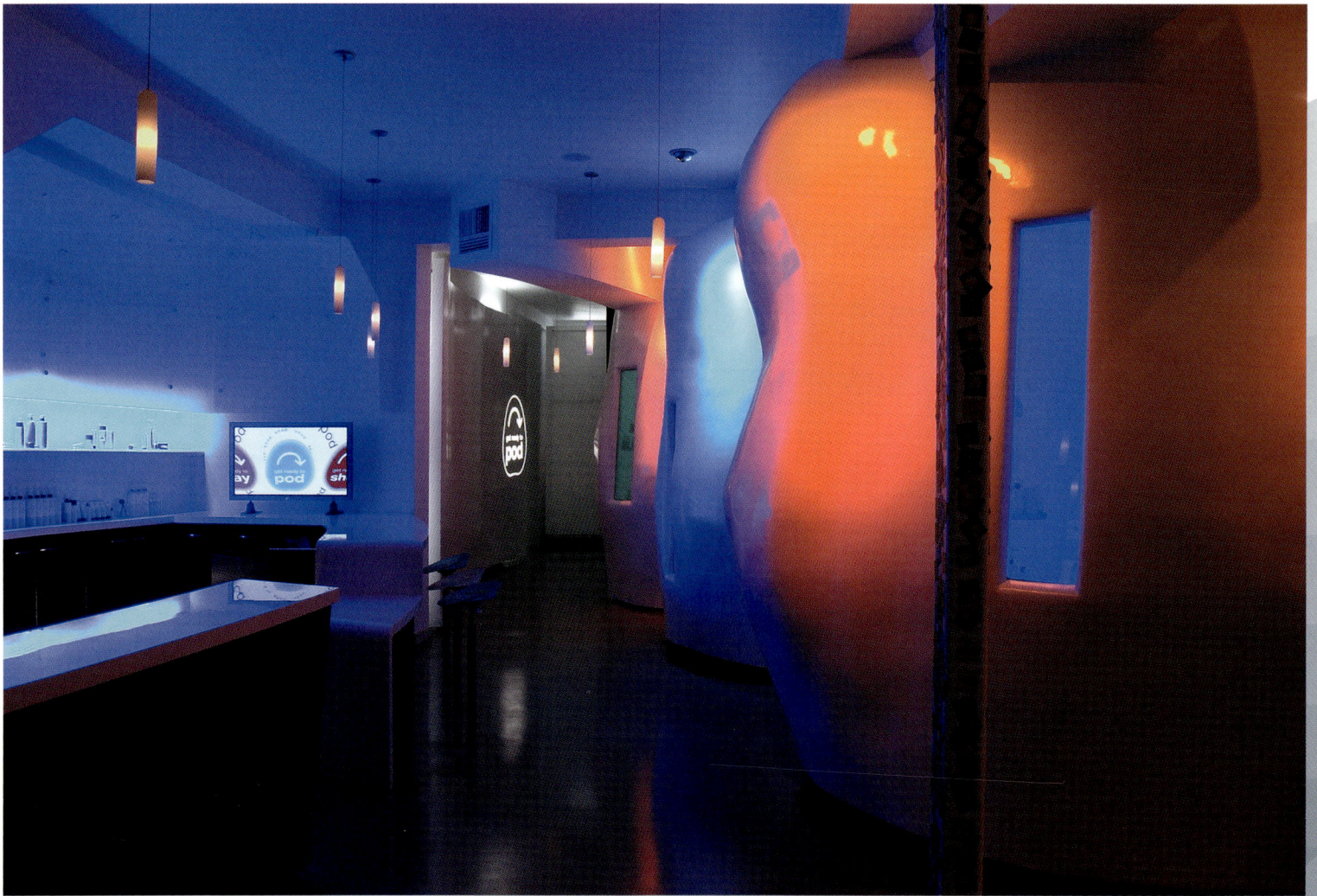

prefers. Mathew Divaris, creative director at Dermalogica, abhors the staples offered at traditional skin-care salons, such as overly thick towels and unflattering robes, which he foregoes in favour of the more modern, sensuous sarong and porous cloths, steam-heated and applied to the body. Inside the pods, Therapist Control Panels allow specially trained staff members to manipulate temperature and light while remaining seated. Just outside the pods, a custom supply galley, reminiscent of those found on aeroplanes, holds all necessities that do not need to be within arm's reach.

To create the pods, a 3-D computer model was generated and subsequently used to determine the curve of each metal stud in the framework of the cubicles. The curvy structures, whose shape is inspired by the plastic nature of human skin, were covered in plasterboard and painted white. Although the space is only some 154 m², the architects wanted to achieve a sense of contrast. To counterbalance the smooth white pods and high-gloss polyurethane floors, for example, a dry-stacked wall of rough concrete tiles was layered 'extra unevenly'. And the sinuous contours of pods and walls complement the straight lines of the existing building. The goal was to give visitors to the centre 'an experience of indulgence before the treatment even begins'.

The gentle ramp, an almost subliminal element that slopes from the front to the rear of the space, was actually born out of necessity. Compliance with local wheelchair-accessibility laws demanded a solution for the two entrances, front and back, which were not level with the original floor. Creating an even slope turned out to be beneficial to both the situation of the pods, which now appear to be hovering, and the overall sequence of motion that the visitor experiences upon entering the premises. After walking in, they move through or around the product display to reach the treatment pods. 'There is a progression from the active public zone with its street connection,' explain the architects, 'to the tranquil and private areas of the pods. We created an animated path that draws the eye deep into the space.'

The unusual relationship between interior and exterior is a special feature of the project. Except for certain materials – smooth plaster surfaces and concrete tiles – used on a small area of the façade to hint at the design of the space inside, the typical 1920s Spanish-Colonial exterior was left intact. The architects installed a 6-m² sliding window that slots into the wall when opened, which is most of the time in warm and sunny Santa Monica. Abramson has seen pedestrians stop in their tracks to examine the unusual scene inside. After closing time, when Dermalogica on Montana is dark, the pods pulsate with coloured light, accentuating the somewhat sci-fi feel of the setting.

↑ At night the pods – pulsating with colour and attracting the attention of passers-by – resemble set pieces from Roger Vadim's Barbarella.

→ Dermalogica's colour-coded packaging prompted the architects to design an interior with a focus on white.

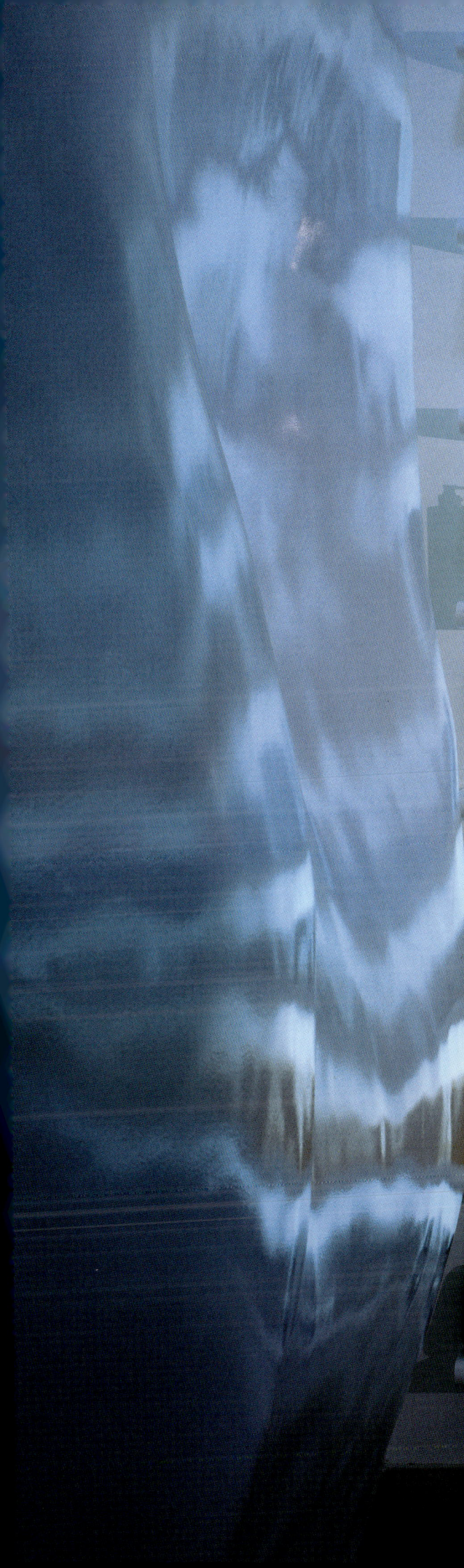

Inspired by the plasticity of human skin, curvaceous white-painted pods seem to hover above the gently sloping floor.

Therapist Control Panels make it easy for specially trained employees working with clients to remain seated while adjusting temperature, light and even music. All nonessential items remain outside the pods.

Abramson has seen *pedestrians stop* in their tracks to examine the unusual scene inside

architect

Abramson Teiger
Architects
8924 Lindblade Street
Culver City, CA 90232
USA
T +1 310 838 8998
douglas@
abramsonteiger.com
www.abramsonteiger.com

photographers

Lars Frazer Photography
lars@larsfrazer.com
www.larsfrazer.com
-
John Linden Photography
john@
johnlindenphotographs.com
www.johnlinden
photographs.com

legend
01 Cashier
02 Wrapping station
03 Changing rooms
04 Treatment pods
05 Lavatories

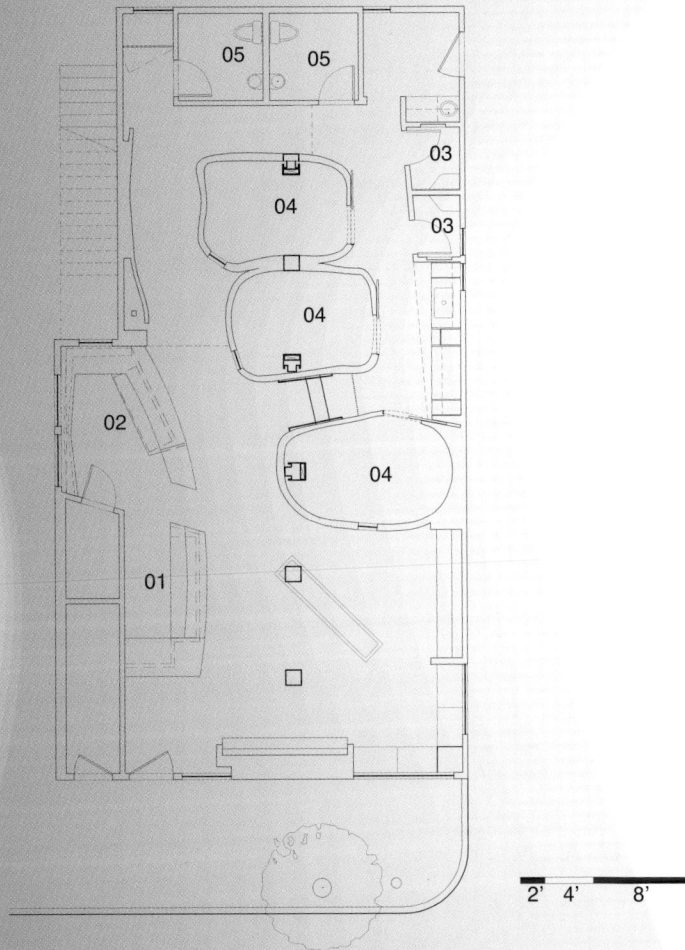

05   05

03

04

03

04

02

04

01

2' 4'   8'

↖ By designing individual pods
for beauty treatments, Abramson
Teiger Architects broke with the
traditional layout of the beauty
salon, which reserves small
rooms at the rear of the interior
for such treatments.

← The minimalist design of
cash desk and packaging area
does nothing to distract from
the pods.

client
Bundy Bundy
manufacturer
Kirchberger Tischlerei
construction
RWT
lighting design
Christian Ploderer

total floor area (m²)
420
duration of construction
3 months
opening
September 2006

project
Bundy Bundy Hair Salon
Lamberg Sprinzenstein
Palace
Wallnerstrasse 3
1010 Vienna
Austria
T +43 1 914 1162
www.bundy.at

gps
N 48°12' E 016°22'

BWM Architekten und Partner

Bundy Bundy Hair Salon

vienna/austria

Text by Stephan Ott

Vienna – the acme of architecture, culture and lifestyle – is home to St Stephan's Cathedral, baroque architecture, palaces, coffee houses, the opera and Hotel Sacher, which serves the famous pastry that bears its name. An exclusive address in the Austrian capital now pampers an international elite.

The scale and quality of Vienna's historical highlights are regarded as unique throughout the world. And the city's current crop of architects and designers are fortunate to have this treasure trove as a source of inspiration. One example is Bundy Bundy's flagship salon, which recently opened on Wallnerstrasse. Founded in 1974 by brothers Hans and Georg Bundy, the establishment is regarded as a Viennese institution whose reputation extends beyond the nation's borders.

The new home of the star stylists' salon is the historic Lamberg-Sprinzer Palace, also called Kaiserhaus, a baroque building owned by the Habsburgs in the mid-18th century. The Bundys commissioned a local firm, BWM Architekten und Partner, to design and realize their new premises.

Taking their lead from the sequence of baroque rooms in the building, the architects assigned each room a specific character. Following the lines of the original architecture and the social functions of these rooms – interiors appropriate for receptions, ceremonies and parties – they designed a series of spaces, modifying the original rooms to accommodate the functions of a hair salon and creating a progression of surprises. Reflecting the concept of 'atmosphere linked to function' are colour contrasts, which include the warm, creamy tone of the lobby, the dark aubergine of the men's salon and the glittering gold of the ladies' salon. Each interior has a lighting scheme tailored to generate a particular ambience.

The architects are enthusiastic. 'Take any hairdressing salon you know or can imagine,' says Erich Bernard of BWM, 'and compare it with the new Bundy salon. This place is worlds apart . . . like a palace, where each

'As we were designing the salon, we focused on *the mood of the interior* and not the function'

«Erich Bernard»

↑ Low seating and floor lamps, purpose-designed for Bundy Bundy, dominate the lounge.

← The prevailing atmosphere at Bundy Bundy emerges from BWM's use of classic materials combined in various ways.

customer can find a favourite spot with a distinctive character.' Usable space in the salon adds up to 420 m², which is divided into two areas: the main salon, which consists of four large, individually designed rooms; and a 'hair spa', which is devoted to hair-care and relaxation. Walls form one huge mirror, which is made up of innumerable fragments of faceted glass in a variety of shapes and tints and which stretches the entire length of all the rooms, linking the different environments. Incorporated into the mirrored wall are showcases and monitors. Clad in tufted leather, the inner surface of the wall lends access to cloakrooms, a powder room and two elegantly appointed 'special treatment' rooms.

Visible throughout the salon are classic materials, used alone or in combination, such as wood, glass, silk and ceramic. 'The atmosphere corresponds to the function and contents of each room,' says Bernard. 'Even so, as we were designing the salon, we focused on the mood of the interior and not the function.'

Grey-tinted mirrors at the entrance hint of the exclusive world about to be entered. Customers are greeted in the reception area as if they were guests in a hotel lobby. The space features a reception desk, a bar, a waiting area and a small shop. Above their heads, displayed on a screen running the entire width of the room, are the latest hair-care products and cosmetics, along with the Bundy logo. This space leads to the lounge, which includes a bar and a fireplace, where customers are invited to relax, to catch up on the latest developments at Bundy Bundy, and to discuss their particular wishes with a stylist.

Aubergine was selected for the men's salon because of its obvious appeal to the target group and its reference to a traditional men's club. The colour and materials used in the low lounge furniture match the flooring. Huge purpose-designed floor lamps with dark shades dominate the high-ceilinged room. The so-called 'trend area' in delicate pink is enhanced by large floral designs modelled on 19th-century French tapestries. In this area, the part of the interior that most resembles a conventional hair salon, customers sit on pink chairs next to the wall. Mirrors can be folded shut like the winged panels of a triptych and transformed into an integral part of the wall. Opening them reveals panels of light. Each seat is screened from those on either side of it.

At the centre of the crystal room, with its iridescent mother-of-pearl walls, is a spacious oval table with a golden surface, which shares the space with deep nacre-hued armchairs. Round, vertically positioned mirrors encircle the tabletop – a nod to the time-honoured salon mirror – completing an ensemble that emphasizes the luxurious atmosphere. Like a glittering waterfall, a sophisticated chandelier descends from ceiling to table. Finally, in the hair spa, described as an 'oasis of wellbeing' for relaxed hair-care, pale-green walls and ceiling promote a sense of freshness and ease. After enjoying the comfort of massage chairs and a view of the peaceful inner courtyard, customers leave the salon feeling regenerated.

↑ The latest products are displayed on an illuminated board running the length of the room.

→ Display cases and monitors are set into a mirrored surface that extends across one wall of the salon.

Elegance and luxury in mother-
of-pearl mark the 'crystal room'.

A delicate wash of pink suffuses
the salon's 'trend area'.

architect
BWM Architekten
und Partner
Margaretenplatz 4/L1
1050 Vienna
Austria
T +43 1 205 9070
office@bwm.at
www.bwm.at

photographer
martin stickler fotografie
martin@sticklerfotografie.nl
www.sticklerfotografie.at

legend
01 Reception
02 Lounge area
03 Changing rooms
04 Trend area
05 Glamour area
06 Spa area
07 Shampoo area
08 Lavatories
09 Storage

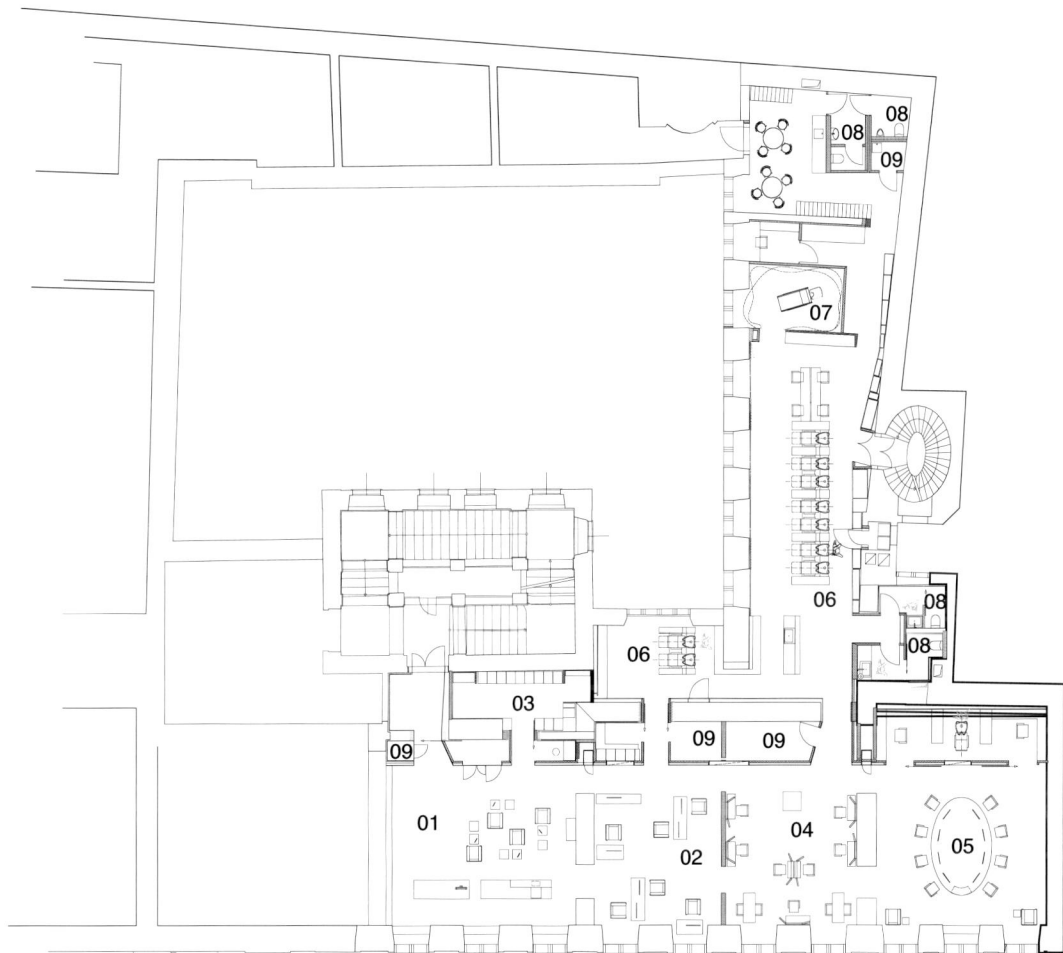

↖ In the hair spa, the focus is on
hair care and relaxation.

← Welcome to the club: the gents'
salon is immersed in a deep
shade of aubergine.

client
Glamour College of Beauty
engineer
Showa civil engineering
manufacturer
SOGO furniture
graphic design
Yuko Furuse

total floor area (m²)
1938
**duration of
construction**
11 months
opening
September 2005

project
Glamour Annex
1-4-8 Nanbanaka Naniwa-ku
Osaka City, Osaka 556-0011
Japan
T +81 6 6649 2013

gps
N 34°39' E 135°28'

Propeller Design
Glamour Annex
osaka/japan

Text by Masaaki Takahashi

Though beauticians may appear to have glamorous jobs, those entering the profession often learn their skills amid rather drab surroundings. The Osaka building housing the new extension to beauty school Glamour, however, is clad in a stunning lacelike exterior, while inside, facilities and eye-catching classrooms are on a par with salon interiors that cater to paying customers.

Glamour College of Beauty boasts the proud reputation of having the highest pass rate of any school participating in Japan's state beautician exams. The college also operates a number of successful hair and nail salons. In 2005, to commemorate its 50th anniversary, the college built an extension – called Glamour Annex – on a site adjacent to its main school building. The complex is located in Osaka's Minami district, a stylish mid-city area that is in the process of regaining its former vitality. Minami's urban-renewal project includes the recent expansion of existing stores, as well as the appearance of large-scale business facilities and department stores.

Yoshihiro Kawasaki, president of Propeller Design and the man responsible for the look of the chain of salons run by Glamour College, designed the new extension. His concept emerged from the notion of metamorphosis. 'Simply put, the work of a beautician is nothing other than the pursuit of beauty. Since this building's raison d'être is the study of ways to achieve this goal, it was vital to incorporate beauty into the design, which I based on the idea that anyone who walks through the doors will be transfigured – and that each student will metamorphose into a true beauty professional,' explains Kawasaki.

The building stands on a narrow site, 37 m in depth, with a frontage only 8 m wide. Despite the limited dimensions, Kawasaki had to create separate entrances for the college and the ground-floor hair salon. Customers enter on the east side and students on the west side. Combining a beauty salon with a technical college made this project more complicated than most. Furthermore, because nearby buildings virtually cover their sites, with no room left over, they threaten to cramp the style of any and all newcomers. The architect thus faced the dilemma of inserting an extension whose presence would be noticed. The onus was on the 30-m-high façade to draw the public gaze. Kawasaki created a glazed exterior that looks like an alabaster box during the day and, after dark, undergoes a quiet transformation until the whole building appears to be cloaked in a lace-embroidered fabric. He achieved the desired effect by installing a curtain wall made from glazed panels that sandwich a 'membrane' decorated with delicate, purpose-designed graphics. The panels not only reinforce the exterior but also form an elegant tracery of filigree, lit from behind, that reflects changing patterns of light inside and outside the building. The pattern blurs the observer's perception of the true scale of the structure,

The door on the right lends
access to a conference room.
The corridor leads to a training
room. Indirect lighting enhances
the spacious ambience.

making it seem more like an art installation than a building. A variety of elements in the interior correspond to the graphic motif decorating the façade.

The various floors accommodate classrooms for teaching hairdressing, nail care and other beauty-salon services. Additional facilities include a complete photo studio in a dual-level atrium, meeting rooms, a make-up room and an office area. The first-floor shampoo room can hold 30 students. The teak surface on the ground floor extends seamlessly up to the ceiling, while a circular glass partition separates the shampoo area from the rest of the space. Since the actual floor area of the salon is not particularly large, Kawasaki boldly lowered the height of the entrance area and raised the ceiling in the main room, creating a space that opens up dramatically as one enters the building. Individual classrooms are found on floors three to six. Used throughout the building, indirect lighting underlines the sought-after sense of continuity. In contemplating the design of Glamour Annex, Kawasaki says that 'it's the expression of a motional side you just don't see in most academic architecture today, which is what gives this building its individuality.'

'I based the design on the idea that anyone who walks through the doors will be transfigured and that each student will metamorphose into a true *beauty professional*'

«Yoshihiro Kawasaki»

↑ In a complete photo studio
   in the building, professional
   photographers shoot student
   work, from spectacular hairdos
   to subtle cosmetic makeovers.

← After dark, the building
   appears to be cloaked in a
   fragile crocheted fabric.

GLAMOUR BEAUTY SALON

Custom-made crystal
chandeliers hang from the
4-m-high teak ceiling.

architect
Propeller Design
Yoshihiro Kawasaki
23-8-204 Kasuga-cho
Ashiya City,
Hyogo 659-0021
Japan
T +81 7 9725 5144
F +81 7 9725 5145
info@propeller-design.com
www.propeller-design.com

photographer
Nacása & Partners
nasa@nacasa.co.jp
www.nacasa.co.jp

legend
01 Waiting area
02 Beauty salon
03 Shampoo booth
04 Styling area
05 Hall
06 Training room
07 Conference room
08 Office
09 Lecture room
10 Make-up room
11 Photo studio

Second floor

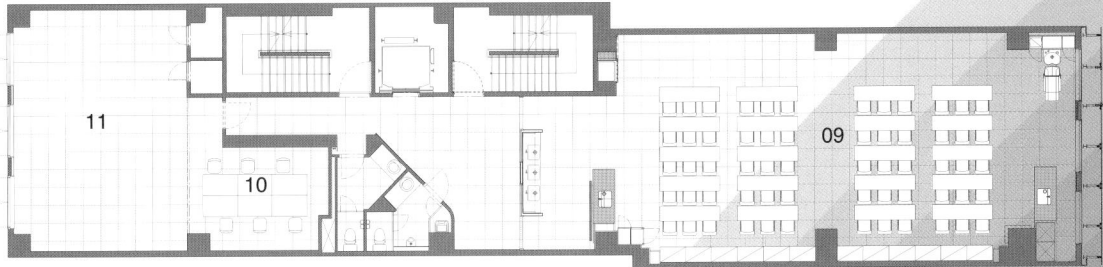

First floor

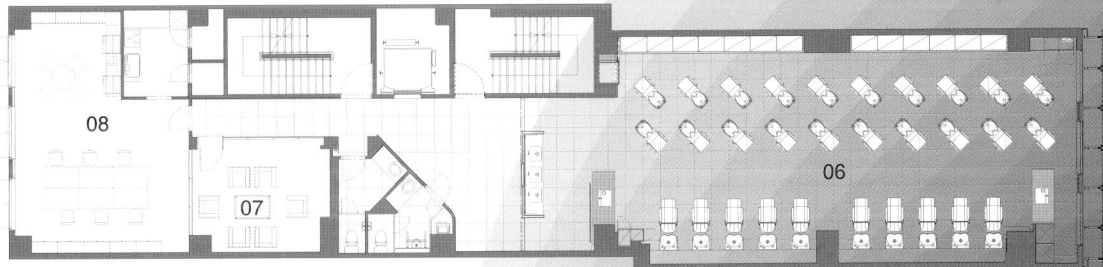

Ground floor

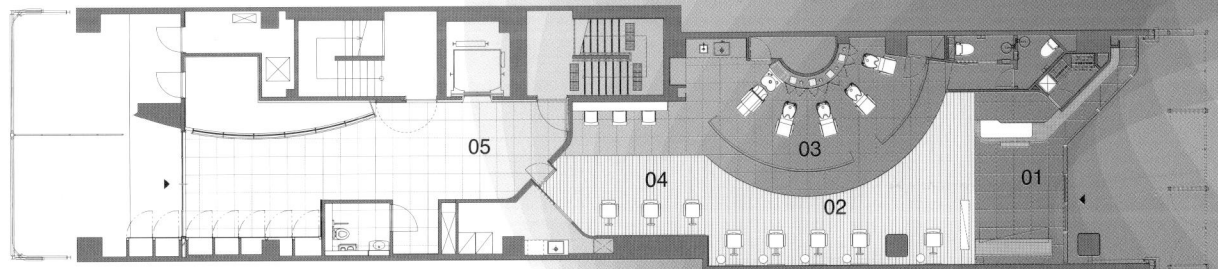

0 1 2   5 meters

↖ Chairs and sinks line the
   shampooing room, where
   differing ceiling heights
   correspond to the various
   functions below.

← In shampooing booths on the
   ground floor, glass partitions
   have been used to create a sense
   of privacy.

client
Peluquería Compagnia della Bellezza

engineer
Mauricio Diego

manufacturers
DADA, Knoll International, Maletti, Hitashi, Ansol and Bang & Olufsen

lighting design
Viabizzuno

capacity
24 clients

total floor area (m²)
160

total cost (€)
350,000

duration of construction
3 months

opening
May 2005

project
Peluquería Compagnia Della Bellezza
Av Sariia 52
Barcelona
Spain
T +34 93 4104 790
www.compagniadella-bellezza.com

gps
N 41°23' E 002°8'

Estudio Minim Vilà & Blanch

Compagnia della Bellezza Hair Salon

barcelona/spain

Text by Sarah Martín Pearson

The Italian glamour that oozes from Compagnia della Bellezza, a worldwide chain of hair salons, dons a new look in Barcelona, where Minim Vilà & Blanch tones down the brand's air of exuberance to create a realm of relaxation geared to the lives of laid-back Barcelonans.

Classy in concept and vivacious in practice, Compagnia della Bellezza – an Italian-based organization with hair salons around the world – asked interior experts Elina Vilà and Agnes Blanch to design its Barcelona outlet, a space that required the client to accept a certain cultural reorientation in terms of both aesthetics and functionality. In many of its salons, the ebullient Italian compagnia polishes the professional skills of its staff within a space pulsing with activity. Against the sounds of hairdryers, chitchat and loud background music – and with the participation of the customers – 'maestros' instruct their apprentices, turning the whole hairdressing experience into nothing less than a live performance. It's a method that may attract customers in certain parts of Italy, but in Barcelona things work differently. The Catalan public appreciates a more discreet approach and a quieter ambience, suffused in contained elegance.

'Our client soon understood the need to temper the original concept and was very eager to listen to what we had to say on the matter,' says Vilà, who recalls envisioning, even at the outset, 'a sober atmosphere' and 'an elegant look'. 'Our model for the aesthetics of the interior was inspired by Claudio Silvestrin's Armani stores.'

For the neutral colour scheme they had in mind, the designers chose three rather austere materials: untreated steel, dark wood and pale-grey porcelain tiles. All remaining surfaces were to be white, with the exception of one dramatic touch of colour: the red wall behind the reception desk. Intended as an eye-catcher to attract passers-by, the wall features a concealed door that slides open, lending access to the toilet area. At street level, the damaged, mosaic-tiled façade of the triangular building was in need of repair. Highlighting the refurbished

Individual floor-to-ceiling work stations visually stretch the space. At the centre of the salon, the maestro displays his skills, offering a live performance.

exterior are large windows outlined in 20-cm-deep steel frames that give the impression of a tunnel. A steel frame of the same type surrounds a mirror above the stone sink in the toilet. At the entrance, a 230-x-240-cm sliding glass door, again framed in steel, leads the way to a reception area furnished with design classics such as Bertoia's Diamond chairs and Saarinen's Tulip coffee table (currently produced by KnollStudio). Bordering this area is a long, custom-designed display unit with built-in lighting and MDF shelving painted white. This volume also serves as a partition, which hides the hair-washing area from public view, guaranteeing the customers' privacy. Colourful products displayed against the luminous background enliven the scene, as do chair cushions and images shown on a flat screen that has been integrated into an adjoining column. The hair-washing area was planned as an independent section of the salon in which customers can enjoy a relaxing experience. Aromatherapy, chromotherapy and soft music add to their pampered sense of indulgence. The toilet area, which also pursues the idea of comfort, has been delicately designed in natural materials and dark colours to provide a cosy yet stylish feeling.

Compagnia della Bellezza offers its clientele an extensive selection of hair-colour products by L'Oreal, whose merchandise is prominently displayed throughout the salon. The hair-colouring zone, a distinctive feature of the interior that can be compared to a laboratory, allows customers to choose from 251 shades. A stainless-steel kitchen isle by Dada includes a system of suspended black-laminate drawers: a perfect furnishing solution for the interior concept. Here the designers clad both floor and walls with porcelain tiling, an easy-to-clean, waterproof surface. The designers were not deterred by the irregular arrangement of the existing premises. 'We used the triangular layout to our own benefit,' says Vilà, 'by positioning the work station of Claudio Bucci (chief hairdresser) at the centre, enabling him to direct the apprentices around him and to put his role as maestro into practice.' The central work station is also suitable for the type of make-up sessions that draw an audience. A comparatively low ceiling (260 cm) inspired the designers to line the façade with individual, floor-to-ceiling work stations clad in dark wood and full-body mirrors that visually stretch the space. The backs of cupboards concealed by these mirrors display neon-lit advertising posters that face the street. This idea corresponds to the brand's highly commercial approach, which emphasizes the use of visual communication. The lighting scheme, a key element in hair salons, includes ceiling lamps that radiate both warm and cool light, a combination that enhances the sheen of hair; and mirror-framing bulbs – like those in theatre dressing rooms – whose warm glow softens facial features by eliminating unwanted shadows. Vilà and Blanch have shaped a Catalan environment with a warm hint of Italy that invites Barcelonans to put up their feet, lean back and unwind.

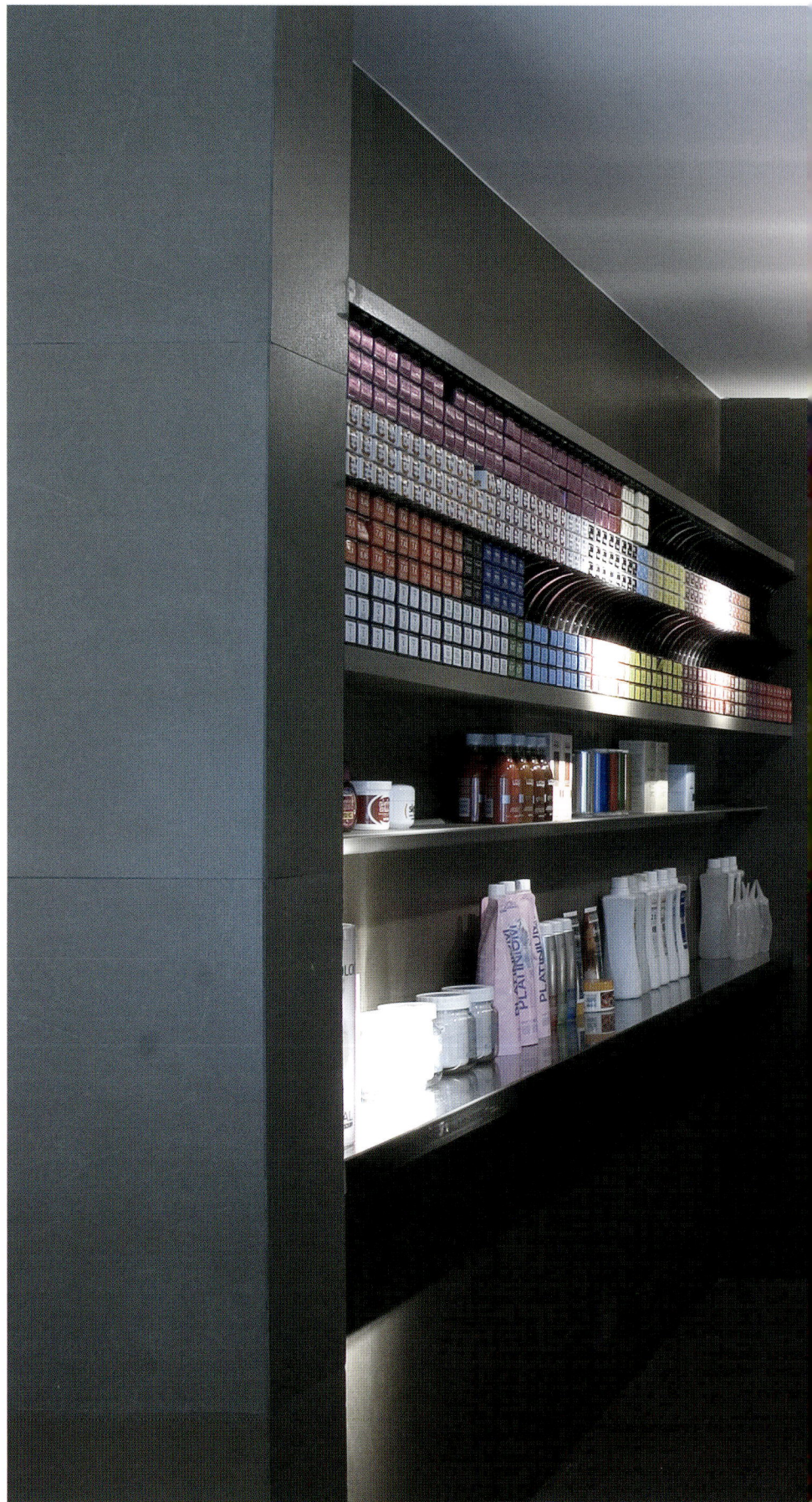

Highlighting the hair-colouring 'laboratory' is a stainless-steel kitchen isle by Dada, which is complemented by easy-to-clean, porcelain-tiled surfaces.

At the centre of the *triangular interior* that characterizes
this elegant hair salon in Barcelona, 'Maestro' Claudio
Bucci supervises the work of his apprentices

↖ A colourful range of cosmetic products is enticingly displayed in a white-painted MDF shelving unit with built-in lighting. The unit borders the waiting area and doubles as a partition, which hides the hair-washing area from public view.

↑ Work stations are clad in dark wood and full-body mirrors. Combined warm and cold lighting enhances hair sheen, while mirror-framing light bulbs soften facial features.

Above the natural-stone washbasin in the toilet area is a large steel-framed mirror: a reference to the steel-framed windows of the façade.

architect
Estudio Minim Vilà & Blanch
Av Diagonal 369
08037 Barcelona
Spain
T +34 93 2722 425
proyectos@
estudiovilablanch.com
www.estudiovilablanch.com

photographer
Stephan Zähring
stephan@zaehring.com
www.maria.com.es

legend
01 Reception
02 Shampoo area
03 Colouring area
04 Styling area
05 Lavatories
06 Storage
07 Office

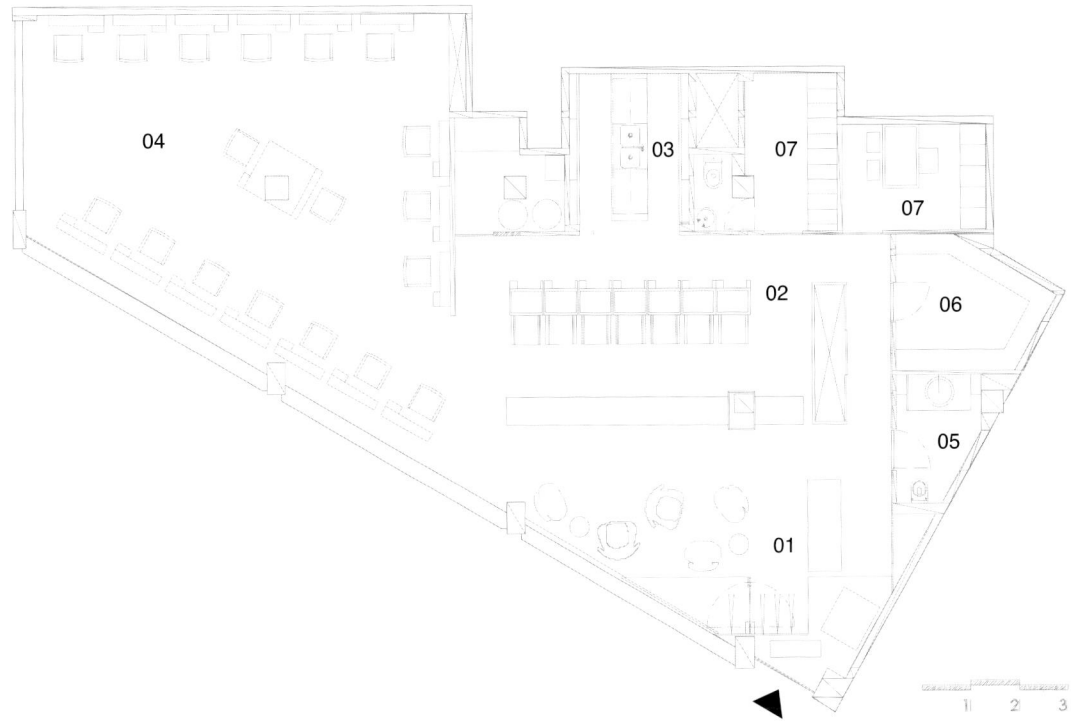

client
Edge Lotus
engineers
Kano Komuten and
Takahashi Industry
manufacturer
Atalia
total floor area (m²)
624

total cost (€)
725,594
budget per m² (€)
1162
duration of construction
8 months
opening
February 2006

project
Edge Lotus Beauty Salon
6-905 Hoshimigaoka
Mie, Kuwana 511-0912
Japan
T +81 5 9433 1333
F +81 5 9433 3331
www.edge-hair.com

gps
N 35°4' E 136°41'

Hiroshi Nakamura

Edge Lotus Beauty Salon

kuwana/japan

Text by Masaaki Takahashi

Hiroshi Nakamura emphasizes an awareness of the space around the body extending 1.5 m in every direction. Distancing himself from traditional architecture governed solely by engineering and technology, he draws on art and cognitive psychology and blends relaxation with stimulation to create environments that delight the senses.

For Edge Lotus, Nakamura conceived a beauty salon that offers to each customer a sense of being cocooned in a private space. Had the designer split the salon into separate rooms, the isolation of each treatment area would have prevented ease of movement and thus had a negative impact on both service and communication among staff members. And had he blocked sightlines with obstacles such as high partitions, customers might have felt as though the walls were pressing in on them. Here, the architect not only resolved such issues but also adopted them as the starting point and theme of his design.

A glance at the floor plan reveals a cluster of smaller areas delineated by organic lines that strongly echo an ant's nest. Not Nakamura's original intention, the pattern evolved naturally during the design process. Separated by curved walls, these spaces are interconnected in a highly fluid way; rather than being an enclosed unit, each space flows freely into the next. 'A number of techniques have been used to make each customer feel as if they're in

their own personal space,' says Nakamura.

Inside the salon, the slope of the floor follows the incline of the building site, descending gradually from the entrance and car park towards the far end of the interior. The height of the partition walls varies accordingly, ranging from 1.4 m at the highest point to 0.5 m at the lowest, making them the perfect height to form bench seating within the waiting area close to the entrance. Elsewhere, the partitions are tall enough to rise above the head of a seated client, while still allowing staff on their feet to cast an eye over the entire salon. By maintaining a unified space above a certain height, the design effectively counters any feeling of claustrophobia. In each area, the walls cleverly assume a different function, from reception desk to bar counter to display board.

Each circular 'cocoon' provides ample room for the beautician to move with ease around a centrally placed chair. Translucent curtains can be drawn around individual booths for the sake of added privacy. When all curtains are drawn, passers-by glancing inside catch sight

↑ Partitions no higher than 1.4 m make it possible for staff to view activities throughout the interior.

← Triggering the curiosity of passers-by are a perforated ceiling, drawn curtains that resemble pillars, and structural columns tilted to function as braces.

Hiroshi Nakamura draws on art and cognitive psychology to create buildings that delight *the senses*

edgelotus

of a cluster of stout, white pillars that show off the interior to great effect, further igniting their curiosity.

The corners of interior walls gently curve, their soft edges painted not white but the faintest of pastels. A close look reveals a palette of delicate shades in gradations of pale green, blue, pink, cream and beige, which melt away the boundaries between floor and walls. Both curves and colours contribute to the light, airy ambience, while obscuring the dimensions of the space and reducing any 'hemmed in' feelings. In psychology, the term 'affordance' is used to describe how features within our immediate environment suggest ways of interacting with what surrounds us. In the case of a room, for example, changes in tangent and texture between wall and floor might be used as clues to measure depth. At Edge Lotus, however, Nakamura has subverted the process of affordance by blurring visual differences in the interior architecture, enveloping visitors in the space and thus encouraging them to relax, while also injecting a note of excitement and expectation as they move through the salon. Supported by delicate columns, the ceiling is an expanse of thin steel sheeting punctuated by countless tiny holes. Some of the columns are vertical, whereas others have been set at an angle to function as braces. Located on a main thoroughfare in Kuwana (Mie Prefecture), the salon occupies a sloping, 764-m² site. Instead of prosaically

squeezing in as many seats as possible, Nakamura opted for a lavish use of space. His arrangement of roomy individual booths within a uniquely designed interior emphasizes the service aspect of the business, downplays cost performance and promises to usher in the implementation of an attractive new business style in the salon sector.

'Today, young Japanese people have an awareness of space that works on two levels: even when they are in public, they have a sense that the space immediately surrounding their bodies is somehow private,' comments Nakamura, who continues to experiment with sensuous environments that complement or stimulate this sensitivity to physical space.

↑ An impressive view of the salon after dark features a logo lit from behind.

→ Gradated pastels blur the boundaries between floor and walls.

Each booth provides ample room for the beautician to move with ease around a centrally positioned chair.

The architect is interested in
stimulating human perception
and in creating an atmosphere
alive with illusionary magic.

architect
NAP Architects
Mr. Hiroshi Nakamura
505 Sky Heights,
3-1-9 Tamagawa,
Setagaya-ku,
Tokyo 158-0094
Japan
T +81 3 3709 7936
nakamura@nakam.info
www.nakam.info

photographers
NAP Architects
Mr. Nobuaki Nakagawa
atsurei@aa.bb-east.ne.jp
Mr. Yoshida
makoto.y@sweet.ocn.ne.jp

legend
01 Reception
02 Wardrobe
03 Waiting area
04 Councelling area
05 Preperatory area
06 Shampoo area
07 Cut area
08 Perm area

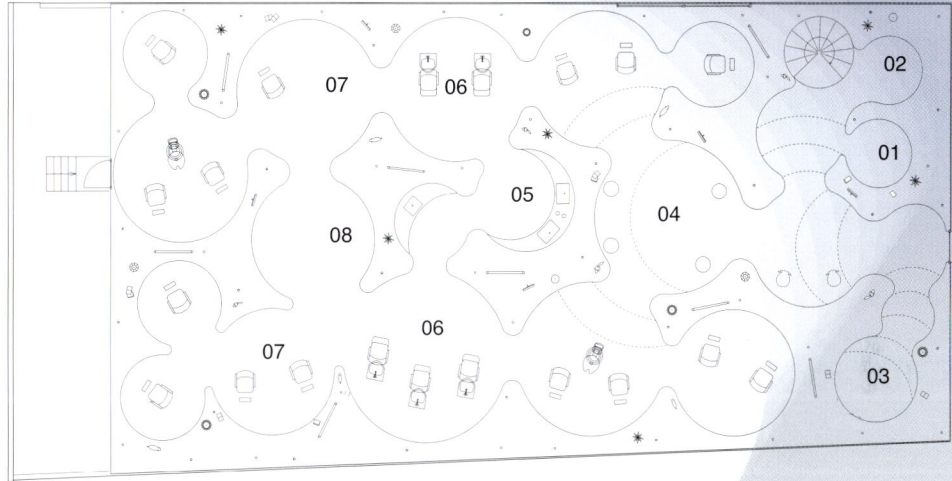

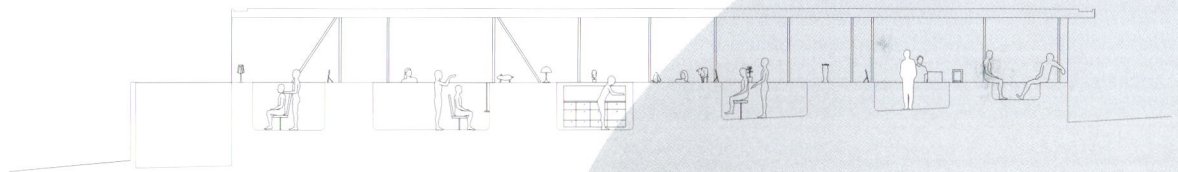

client
Jürg Sandmeier
manufacturer
Bene Büromöbel
capacity
12 clients
total floor area (m²)
100

total cost (€)
85,000
duration of construction
10 days
opening
June 2006

project
Coiffure Art Team
Spalenberg 2
4051 Basel
Switzerland
T +41 61 263 3388
info@artteam.ch
www.art-team.ch

gps
N 47°33' E 007°35'

Fumiko Gotô
Coiffure Art Team
basel/switzerland

Text by Stephan Ott

Strolling around Basel's old town keeps residents in good shape. Steep paths wind from the Rhine valley up the hillsides of Spalenberg and Nadelberg, for example. Beautiful surroundings include lovingly designed galleries, theatres and shops – and, at the heart of the old town, the Coiffure Art Team salon.

Need pampering? In Basel, the place to be is Spalenberg 2. Founded in 2001 by Jürg Sandmeier, the Coiffure Art Team salon is housed under the same roof as Stampa, a gallery and art bookshop that walked off with Basel's Kulturpreis in 2006. In the summer of 2006, the salon celebrated its fifth birthday by giving itself a new look. The 100-m² interior was completely redesigned at a total cost of Euro 85,000. Realization took just a fraction over ten days. From the start, the design was not about exclusive materials and picture-perfect premises in which everything matched, right down to the smallest detail. Patrons were to be immersed in an ambience that would blend in with the old town while also allowing plenty of room for a playful contrast of form and colour. With this aim in mind, Sandmeier went on a search for simplification, following a trend that's recently been dominating much of interior design in this part of Europe. He joined forces with Fumiko Gotô, a Japanese-born architect who lives in Switzerland. The idea was to simplify not only the use of high-tech products, but also the overall design of the interior.

Approaching the project as an architect, Gotô wanted 'to create an effect and make an impressionistic impact' in much the same way as a set designer working in the theatre, 'using widely available and inexpensive materials like chipboard and MDF'. As it turned out, the reference to theatre covered both materials and the overall atmosphere of the salon. Keeping in mind the work of set designers, Gotô created 'a stage on which hair stylists become performers and clients spectators'. The latter 'look into the mirror and observe the act of transformation' as it's happening to them. Incorporated into the 'stage' – a folded element that looks like something made from origami paper – are mirrors, footrests and a long counter. Practical items for daily use are stored in a large closet that runs the entire length of the salon.

Gotô's use of an origami-like element reflects another current trend: a return to traditional forms and ornaments. Increasingly, it is the architect rather than the designer who contemplates ways of dealing with a world that is becoming progressively more virtual and thus 'disembodied'. Japanese origami, so rich in tradition, has

In a salon that doubles as a stage, customers can follow every move in the mirror on the wall.

long since outgrown its limited definition as a handicraft requiring patience and dexterity. Currently, the Japanese art of paper folding is helping technologists, architects and inventors to solve highly complicated problems. Origami serves as a basis for everything from folded street maps and airbags to the solar panels used on satellites.

Like most Japanese children, Gotô mastered the art of origami folding at an early age. In her design for the hair salon, she has done more than simply delve into the origins of paper folding. She has taken her interpretation of origami to an even higher level by exploring the theme of *unfolding*. Visitors to the salon can follow their metamorphoses in the mirror, quite traditionally, and the unfolded wall, which symbolizes such transformations, underlines their reason for being in the salon. With a new haircut, we not only change our appearance but also gain a fresh sense of self-awareness and assurance. The salon has a total of 12 'unfolding', transformational spaces. The chairs appropriately come from the Rondo series made by Austrian furniture manufacturer Bene. With their two organically shaped, smartly joined wooden shells, they perfectly complement the wall design, whose stylistic elements rely on technology.

Colours in the salon are restricted to black and white,

a palette that enhances and celebrates the patron's own hair colour and make-up. Vivid yellow is used as a highlight, both in the architecture and on Coiffure Art Team's business cards, price lists and other printed matter. When the salon has closed for the night, a long screen on which media artists' work is projected is rolled down from a slit in the origami 'fold'. Passing pedestrians can view the screen through the salon's yellow window frames. Even when it is closed, the Coiffure Art Team salon melts seamlessly into the cityscape, much to the enjoyment of theatregoers, people out for an evening stroll and perhaps even those with appointments for new hairstyles the following day.

↑ Rondo chairs by Austrian manufacturer Bene Büromöbel enhance the interior.

→ In her design for the hair salon, architect Fumiko Gotô drew inspiration from origami, the art of Japanese paper folding.

134

ART TEAM ©

Japanese origami, so rich in
tradition, has long since outgrown
its limited definition as a *handicraft
requiring patience and dexterity*

↑   Lucid, simple forms throughout
     the space radiate an overall sense
     of calm.

→   The interior concept is reflected
     in the form, colour and material
     of every element and accessory
     in the salon.

architect
Fumiko Gotô
Birmannsgasse 12A
4055 Basel
Switzerland
T +41 61 274 0075
F +41 61 274 0075
f.goto@dplanet.ch
www.fumiko-goto.ch

photographer
Hanspeter Schiess
hanspeterschiess@
bluewin.ch
www.nextroom.at

legend
01 Reception
02 Salon
03 Colour-mixing lab

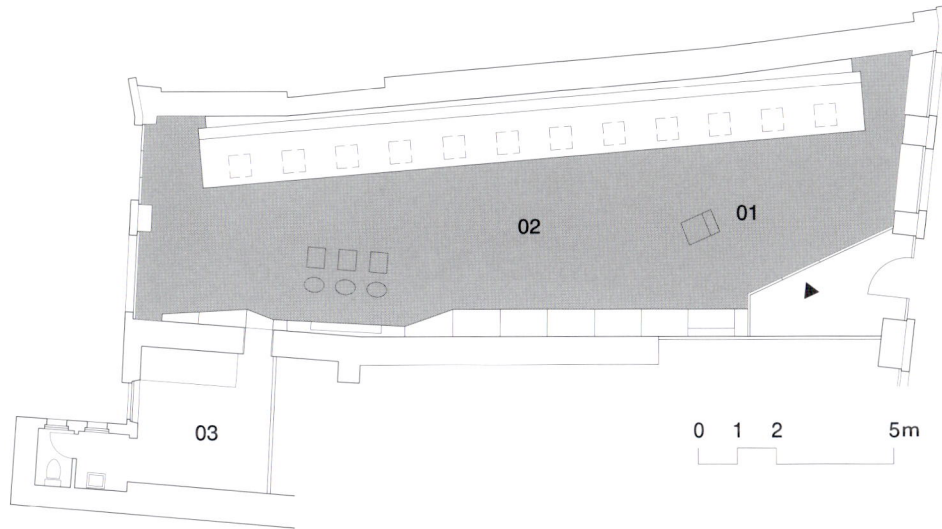

client
Eternal
lighting consultant
ITL
engineer
Sogo Consultants
manufacturer
Bill Gates

total floor area (m²)
347.5
duration of construction
2 months
opening
November 2005

project
Xel-Ha by afloat
5-3-2 Minami Aoyama,
Minato-ku
Tokyo 107-0062
Japan
T +81 3 5766 4171
www.afloat.co.jp

gps
N 35°39' E139°44'

Jun Aoki & Associates

Xel-Ha by afloat

tokyo/japan

Text by Masaaki Takahashi

A ceiling featuring fluorescent lighting and tightly clustered curls is calculated not only to produce an interior with a heavenly glow, but also to give the space a dramatic presence, offsetting its location in a building with a look so distinctive it almost overwhelms the interiors.

Construction on The Jewels of Aoyama was completed in 2005. The project is adjacent to Prada's Herzog & de Meuron-designed Aoyama store on a street in Omotesando, a major Tokyo fashion district. Created by Jun Mitsui & Associates Architects, the development consists of two highly distinctive buildings, one behind the other. Perhaps the architects opted for such unique designs because of the proximity of the now-iconic Herzog & de Meuron edifice. One of the newer buildings is a glass-fronted structure consisting of one floor below ground and two above. Fittingly enough, since it has Cartier as a tenant, its shape is reminiscent of a distorted jewel with a rather cartoonish look. The second stands slightly taller, at four storeys high. Covered in vertical limestone louvres that bring to mind massive chopsticks, it seems to consist entirely of exaggerated vertical lines. Occupying the third floor is Xel-Ha by afloat, a beauty salon positioned directly beneath fine-dining restaurant Pierre Gagnaire à Tokyo.

A major problem faced by the interior designer was how to deal with the fence-like limestone louvres that punctuate the panes of every window. Architect Jun Aoki, the man responsible for the design, set out to craft an interior with a charm that could hold its own among its ultra-striking surroundings. Highlighting his concept is an extraordinary ceiling composed of 750 fluorescent bulbs encircled in swirls of 0.3-mm-thick Walon paper. These reflectors hang at unequal distances from the ceiling – from 130 mm to 500 mm – thus adding variety to the surface. Walon is a durable material often used in lampshades; it consists of natural, Japanese-style paper that has been laminated on both sides with vinyl chloride. At Xel-Ha by afloat, it radiates the kind of light you'd expect from paper lanterns. The result is a softly glowing ceiling. This luminous surface diffuses light throughout the interior, leaving not a single shadow. When you look up at the building at night, the salon appears to be filled with light-emanating bubbles. The effect is beautiful. Although Aoki uses the word 'frills' to describe the illuminative overhead surface, the pattern also suggests

↑ To balance the dominant vertical lines of existing window louvres, the architect used equally strong elements in the interior.

← The eye-catching ceiling features fluorescent lamps that 'bubble' across the overhead surface in a swirling sea of curls.

When you look up at the building at night, the salon appears to be filled with *light-emanating bubbles* that create a beautiful effect

clouds and, more significantly for a salon interior, curls. The ceiling forms an excellent contrast to the bare concrete walls and dark tones of the cork flooring, lockers and counters beneath.

Aoki has emphasized the contrast between the labour-intensive aspects of the design, such as the ceiling ornamentation, and those that required much less trouble on his part, such as the standard materials used for the floor. The outcome of his efforts is an interior that, despite its location in a highly individualistic environment, possesses a strong identity of its own.

The owner of the salon is Hiroki Miyamura, who is well known in Japan as both an aesthetician to the stars and a charismatic personality in his own right. This large-scale establishment, with a staff of about 40 employees, is based on a concept – and an excellent selling point – envisioned by Miyamura, whose idea embraces a comprehensive spectrum of beauty treatments and services, including aromatherapy, healing germanium baths and reflexology. To achieve Miyamura's goal, the salon has been equipped with a head-spa massager, nail-care treatment areas and a VIP room.

The design satisfies the client's desire for a salon interior that blends the luxurious with the casual. The long counter in the reception area, for example, is modelled on a hotel reception desk of the type that offers plenty of storage space. One side of the line of lockers that form a partition dividing the space is monogrammed with the Xel-Ha logo. Flooded with natural light, the main salon features a tidy row of mirrors and chairs that were created by Aoki. The designer placed great emphasis on functionality in the design of these chairs, which reduce stress placed on the body by remaining seated for long periods. With respect to the name, *xel-ha* is a Mayan word meaning 'the place where water collects.' The owner chose this name to signify that his salon would act as a gathering place for people with a highly developed sense of beauty.

↑ A partition between the hairdressing and shampooing areas creates a line of lockers; the monogram is associated with the design of a classy wardrobe trunk.

→ In this shampooing area, a beaming white ceiling forms a striking contrast to the dark cabinet, the dark-brown chairs and the rough surface of the walls.

The interior is filled with a
uniform level of light. The wall
is made of wood-wool cement
boards.

architect

Jun Aoki & Associates
#701, 3-38-11 Jingumae,
Shibuya-ku
Tokyo 150-0001
Japan
T +81 3 5414 3471
info@aokijun.com
www.aokijun.com

photographer

Daici Ano
ano@fwdinc.jp

legend

01 Reception
02 Waiting area
03 Shampoo area
04 Cutting area
05 Cold space
06 Spa
07 VIP room
08 Nail salon
09 Changing room
10 Shower
11 Lavatories
12 Storage
13 Balcony
14 Rear garden

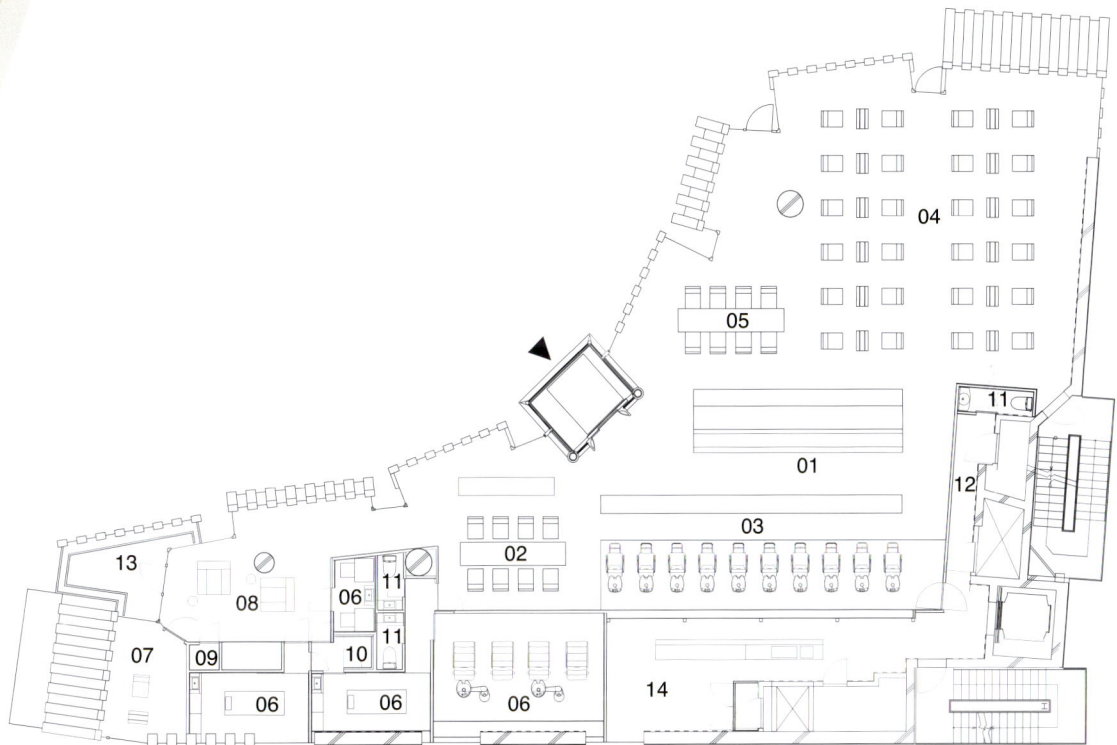

↖ Reflectors on the 750 ceiling
lamps are crafted from
0.3-mm-thick Walon paper, a
product laminated on both sides
with vinyl-chloride resin.

← Every shiny surface in the
interior multiplies the ringlets
that cover the ceiling.

← Curls reflected in mirrors
throughout the space encourage
customers to escape from reality.

client
Bumble and bumble.
contractor
Alliance Builders
consultants
Conversano Associates,
Fisher Marantz Stone and
Shen Milsom & Wilke
engineers
Ambrosino Depinto &
Schmieder and Gilsanz
Murray Steficek

total floor area (m²)
16,000 (total), 5300 (salon)
salon capacity
40 clients
**duration of
construction**
2 years
salon opening
2004

project
The House of Bumble.
415 West 13th St.
New York, NY 10014
USA
T +1 917 606 5000
F +1 917 606 5055
pr@bumbleandbumble.com
www.bumbleand-
bumble.com

gps
N 40°44' E -74°0'

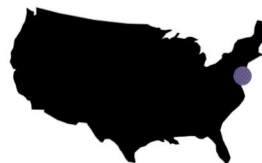

Anderson Architects

The House of Bumble.

new york/usa

Text by Chris Scott

Bumble and bumble came into existence 30 years ago, when founder Michael Gordon opened a salon in midtown Manhattan. By 1992 Bb. had developed its own high-end hair products, complemented by distinctive packaging and the firm's much-admired training programme.

At a certain point, three decades of growth and success had necessitated expansion for Bumble and bumble, a cutting-edge hair-product company and salon based in New York City. Bb. required a place in which all parts of the organization – salon, academy, administrative and creative offices – could be experienced together within a corporate headquarters. It was important to find a space that would be sympathetic to the needs and different to the norm. In 2002, Bb. found the envisioned building in the city's Meatpacking District. Important structural work – the addition of five storeys to the existing three – was needed before the interior could be tackled. It was a mega operation with an overwhelming 16,000 m² and a limited budget. The choice fell on Anderson Architects, with whom Bb. had worked to create its original salon. The architects enthusiastically set to work, fully aware that the project included a complex

programme with an aggressive schedule. Two years later, the House of Bumble opened its doors. The top floor, marked by a white reception desk from USM and double-height windows that admit natural light, is an exclusive retail destination. Furniture and fixtures are a combination of old and new: comfortable leather seating, Mart chairs from B&B Italia, felt-upholstered Quick sofas from Cappellini, walnut cladding, pine trestle tables and industrial trolleys. The main lighting fixture on this floor is an impressive custom-built chandelier. Apart from Bb. products, we find made-to-measure English tailoring by Timothy Everest, with a fitting room inspired by an image of an early-20th-century tailor's shop; Mariage Frères teas; luxury leather accessories; a fine collection of limited-edition goods; a selection of books and magazines; and the Bb. Tea café, where the food is a delight to both palate and eyes, as well as a further temptation to linger. Your

Patrons enjoy a selection of magazines while waiting for the metamorphosis brought about by a new hairstyle, perhaps in a different colour.

appointment at the hair salon, however, is one floor down. A short descent via an open wood-and-steel stairway. Unlike others in its genre, the state-of-the-art salon on the seventh floor is a modern, light-filled, minimalist space with maximum views. Freestanding revolving chairs face the windows, and the spectacular view of the city is undeniably better than any mirror could ever be. Forget what's going on around your head, trust the hair stylist, and confidence – plus a good outcome – is guaranteed. Colouring takes place in a separate area or 'box', which boasts a Barrisol stretch ceiling with built-in lighting that simulates daylight, a factor vital to colourists. The customer sits at a central, communal, 10-m-long stainless-steel table – surrounded by magazines – while overhead heaters allow colours applied to her head to do their job. Cabinets holding products and towels have been finished in a 'hair-dye-proof' car paint, and industrial stainless-steel trolleys were selected for durability and easy maintenance.

Vast numbers of students use the training-salon facilities on floors three and six, where all materials were specially selected to withstand the intensive traffic and the chemicals used. Anderson Architects sealed the concrete floors on these levels for the same reason. An auditorium designed to hold the maximum number of people permitted for assembly on a floor this size, just over 100,

is used for educational purposes, company meetings and events. Lighting had to be flexible to allow for both hair-cutting demonstrations and video projections. Niches created in the outer wall of the auditorium and finished in plywood serve as a gallery, showcasing Bb.'s position at the forefront of hair design.

Offices are found on floors four and five, where the brief asked for a space as open and as interchangeable as possible. At the centre of each floor is a spacious meeting area furnished with Vitra workstations that branch out towards the windows. Here, the size of the floors and the growth of staff called for the design of freestanding 'office huts' that generate privacy while also allowing close interaction among team members. Translucent windows let daylight into these spaces and simultaneously reinforce the desired sense of seclusion.

The first and second floors accommodate independent art galleries, and the basement level has been reserved for a number of the firm's practical facilities. A tented roof garden, to be used for photo shoots and as studio space, is a possible addition. A neutral palette and a minimalist décor unite six floors in which ambience and activities provide the colour. In brief, The House of Bumble is a total, visual, aesthetic New York City experience – and a great place to get a pretty cool hairdo.

↑ Bumble and bumble hair products are set apart by their distinctive, stylish packaging.

→ The ultramodern hair salon on the seventh floor is not only a workplace, but also a vantage point that provides a fantastic view of New York City.

On the eighth and top
floor, a reception area is
complemented by an impeccable
array of aesthetically displayed
merchandise.

The House of Bumble. Is a
total, visual, aesthetic New
York City experience - *and
a great place to get a pretty
cool hairdo*

↑ Tools of the trade.

→ As seen on the eighth floor, the
Bb. logo has been used cleverly
throughout the interior as a
decorative element.

architect

Anderson Architects
555 West 25th St.
New York, NY 10001
USA
T +1 212 620 0996
F +1 212 620 5299
info@andersonarch.com
www.andersonarch.com

photographer

Yoko Inoue
www.yokophoto.com

legend

01 Shampoo area
02 Cutting stations
03 Colour-mixing lab
04 Colour table
05 VIP room
06 Finishing stations
07 Changing room
08 Pamper room

Seventh floor

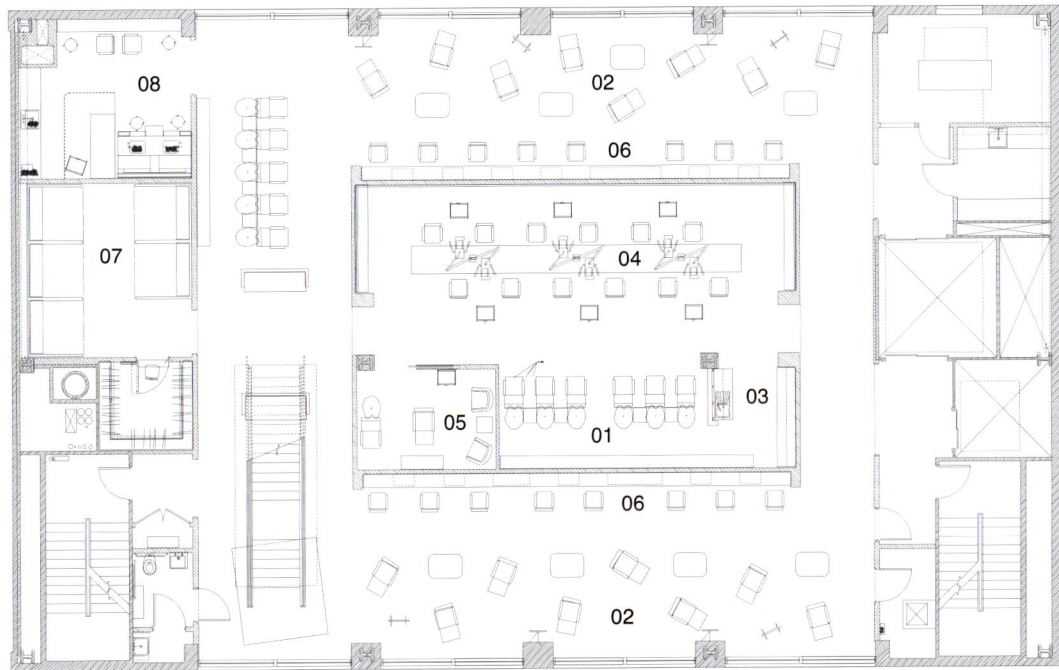

5' 10' 20'

client
Dennis Paphitis and
Clement Yang
engineer
Yao-hung
total floor area (m²)
50
total cost ($)
50,000

budget per m² ($)
1000
**duration of
construction**
1 month
opening
May 2006

project
Aesop Taipei Breeze
Centre
No 39 Fu-shin South Road
Da-an District, Taipei
Taiwan
T +886 2 8772 7767
www.aesop-taiwan.com

gps
N 25°2' E 121°27'

CJ Studio

Aesop, Breeze Centre

taipei/taiwan

Text by Masaaki Takahashi

Purchasers of cosmetics and beauty treatments are showing an increasing interest in products with an organic pedigree. Not satisfied with unsophisticated products that simply avoid chemicals, however, they seek goods and services backed by science and sold in outlets whose images match their high-tech expectations.

From small beginnings in a hair salon in Melbourne, Australia, botanical cosmetic company Aesop has seen its popularity spread in a wave throughout the globe. One sure-fire sign of its success is the number of celebrities in countries all over the world who list its products among their favourites. The range of cosmetics offered by the company contains absolutely no artificial colours or fragrances; nor does it make use of animal and mineral oils. Instead, Aesop's owners insist on formulating their products exclusively from natural ingredients that have been derived from plant extracts. The firm offers a cornucopia of products for the whole body – skin, hair, body, fragrance – which are complemented by a total-care ethos that also places importance on diet and nutrition. Aesop's products are sold in plain glass bottles whose simple shape and clear, dark-amber hue instantly bring medicine bottles to mind. The choice of container was informed by the company policy to reduce the impact on the environment by using recyclable materials and

has had an enthusiastic response from consumers happy to support such initiatives. Taiwanese shoppers who are looking to splash out on Aesop treatments now have the choice of four stores, three of which are in Taipei. One of these is on the ground floor of the Breeze Centre. This gigantic shopping mall is situated at the heart of the metropolis. Boasting 11 levels and a floor space of 7700 m², Breeze Centre has been designed to appeal particularly to women who live in the city or who have travelled to Taipei to partake of the delights the capital has to offer. For this reason, the designers of the mall focused on two main selling points: they created an American-style retail space that offers the quality of service and attention to detail typical of Japanese stores. The Aesop store, part of which accommodates a room for facial treatments, occupies a 50-m² ground-floor unit of the shopping paradise. 'I created a fusion of two brand concepts – "library" and "laboratory" – to generate an atmosphere that would make Aesop stand out from

Aesop is the first cosmetics company to feature kitchen taps in its retail outlets. The spatial layout of the stores is ideal for consultations.

other stores,' says Taipei-based Shichieh Lu of CJ Studio. This versatile designer and architect has worked in a wide variety of creative disciplines. For his design of the Aesop store, he kept the walls white and used indirect lighting to fill the space with a soft light that immediately has a soothing effect on the customer.

The major display units in the store are in the form of three metal 'bookshelves' suspended from the ceiling. In line with the design concept, simple rows of bottles line both these shelves and those along the walls. Each set of shelves is paired with a long 'reading table' that stands below them and to the left as the visitor enters the premises. The spatial layout is ideal for consultations with staff members and for the sampling of products. Positioned on one side of the bookshelves is a 'feature wall' constructed from panels of white, spray-painted metal. A perforated pattern on these panels, which are lit from behind, gives an impression of falling rain. Light shining through the wall creates a glowing motif that represents the flow of both water and information, thus imparting a subtly intellectual atmosphere to the space. What's more, the clean shapes, spotless surfaces and minimalist tones of the interior emphasize a level of hygiene that matches the flawless image of the company.

The recent tendency for consumers to look for minimalist, high-tech design in their preferred hair and beauty salons is handsomely expressed in Lu's interior. A 14-m² room provides the shop's royal clientele with facial treatments, but the facility is also available upon request to the more ordinary among us. Inside this simple room, Lu intriguingly installed an antique barber chair, which reinforces the balanced blend of a LOHAS (Lifestyles of Health and Sustainability) atmosphere and a cutting-edge environment. The overall result is a universal look with the feel of a high-tech research lab. A fitting backdrop for the products, the interior highlights their natural purity in a way that will no doubt attract a sizable clientele to Aesop's new Taipei outlet.

'I created a fusion of two brand concepts – *"library" and "laboratory"* – to generate an atmosphere that would make Aesop stand out from other stores'
«Shichieh Lu»

Slender metal 'bookshelves' holding hundreds of medicine bottles enhance the shop's highbrow atmosphere.

A view from the public corridor.

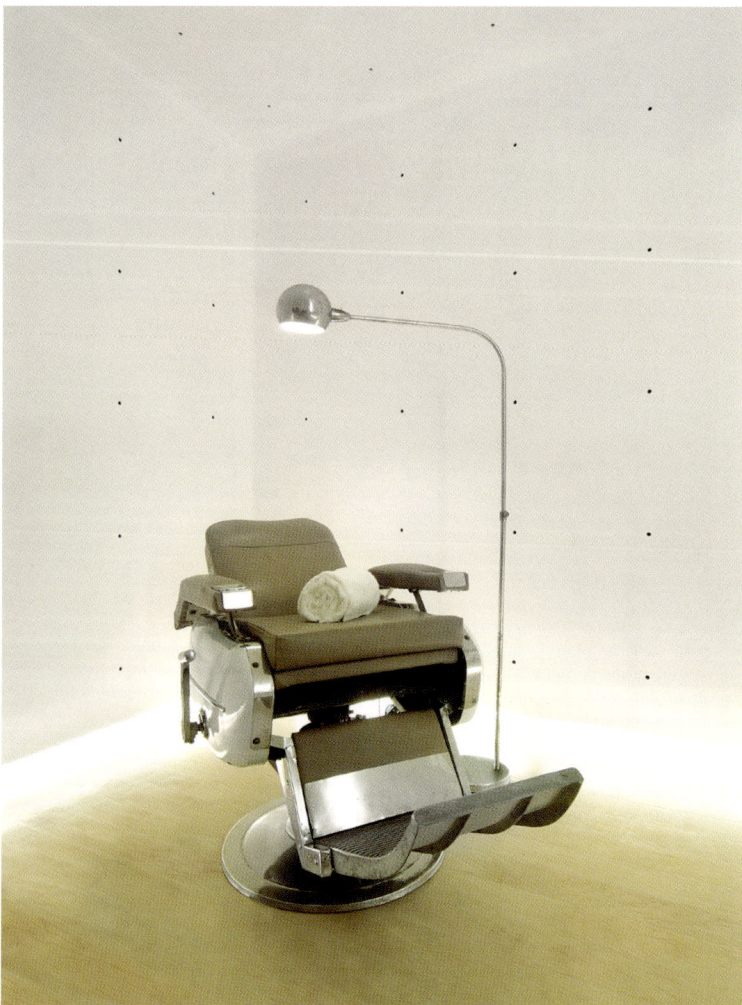

↑ Small holes (1.2 cm) that resemble raindrops are lit from behind. A door to the treatment room is integrated into the wall.

← An antique barber chair at the centre of the treatment room is accompanied by a '60s-style floor lamp. CJ Studio added an oak floor and a white walls to create an otherworldly atmosphere.

architect
CJ Studio
Floor 6 No 54
Lane 260 Kwang Fu
South Road
Taipei 106
Taiwan
T +886 2 2773 8366
cj@shi-chieh-lu.com
www.shi-chieh-lu.com

photographer
Marc Gerritsen
marc@marcgerritsen.com
www.marcgerritsen.com

legend
01 Treatment area
02 Shop

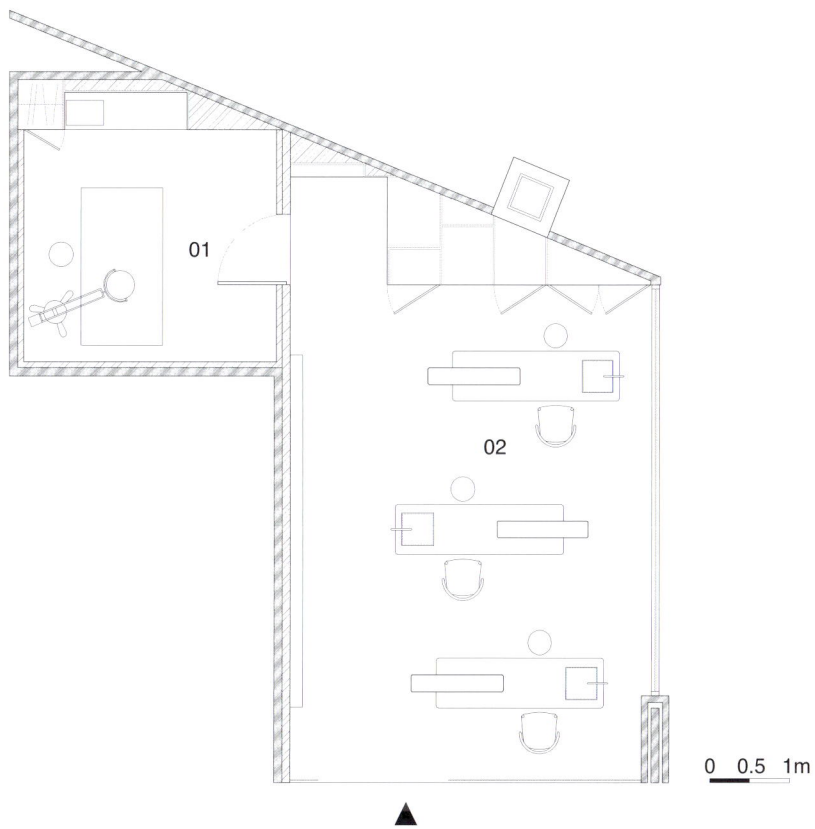

0 0.5 1m

client
Less Is More (LIM)
consultants
EXTEND
engineers
D3
manufacturers
Vitra, Takara Belmont and
Endo Lighting

graphic design
WIPE inc.
total floor area (m²)
77
**duration of
construction**
1 month
opening
October 2006

project
LIM Hair clinie
FLEG Nakameguro B1
1-20-2, Aobadai
Tokyo 153-0042
Japan
T +81 3 5489 5655
clinie@1cs.jp
www.lessismore.co.jp

gps
N 35°43' E 139°44'

Isolation Unit
LIM Hair clinie
tokyo/japan

Text by Chris Scott

In a new Tokyo hair salon designed by Teruhiro Yanagihara of Isolation Unit, minimalism is taken to an extreme, making it immediately evident that LIM stands for 'less is more'. To achieve the desired result, the client opted for a designer known for creating cleaned-lined, spare simplicity.

Top stylist and director of LIM, Kantaro Suzuki, was already managing three salons in Osaka when he chose a location in Nakameguro – a newly developed area in Tokyo that is rapidly becoming the city's number-one place to see and be seen – as a spot for another LIM outlet. Wanting the new salon to be different from the previous three, he envisioned a place where privacy and communication would be of prime importance and where the patron would be given an even more personal type of service: a level of attention similar to the care one receives when seeing a doctor. He coined a special word for his innovative concept by combining 'clinic' and 'creation' to make 'clinie'.

Teruhiro Yanagihara of Isolation Unit, who designs both products and interiors, needed only one month to implement the idea. His initial inspiration came from boxes. He created four rather compact boxes, each of which functions as a private consultation cubicle intended to give an individual a sense of being counselled in the best possible way. According to Yanagihara, the space contains 'no unimportant elements'. He says everything in the design is 'functional, essential and minimalist'.

The LIM Hair clinie is located on the basement level of a shopping centre featuring high-fashion boutiques. At the bottom of the stairs, visitors are greeted by a receptionist whose austere desk in galvanized metal was designed by Yanagihara especially for this venue. Following check-in, their coats are hung in specially designed white fabric bags, while handbags are temporarily stored in a wooden box next to the desk. It's all part of LIM's 'clean and tidy' aesthetic.

Leaving her personal possessions behind, the patron proceeds along a rather dimly lit passageway to the 10-m² 'shampooing box', a space equipped with the bare essentials: two state-of-the-art hair-washing seats by Takara Belmont. She lies back, and the treatment commences. After shampooing, she is taken to one of two 15-m² 'cutting and styling boxes', which contain few objects to distract the eye. Prior to having her hair cut, she receives personalized advice about hair styles; a hair check-up, which includes a microscopic examination of the condition of her hair; and information concerning health and lifestyle habits. Two chairs designed by Maarten Van Severen take a central position within the room, and a huge mirror is propped against the wall. There is little to focus on except what's happening on top of the head, where a member of the LIM staff is busy 'doctoring' the patron's hair. Magazines hang on the rungs of a ladder, also propped against the wall, and a plain wooden shelf holds books. Clearly, there's no tolerance for

Clearly, there's
no tolerance for
clutter
in this room

↑   View of the sparsely furnished
    hair-cutting box.

←   A bare passageway in shades of
    grey leads to the cubicles.

clutter in this room. Within the total space – measuring 77 m², with a ceiling height of 3 m – each of the four boxes, which are separated by 1.8-m high plasterboard partition walls, rests on a platform 30 cm above the floor, a design intervention that permits the stylist to observe activity elsewhere in the salon. The staff room has slightly higher partitions, which allow employees taking a break to be undisturbed by visual activity outside this haven of rest. Yanagihara applied a colour scheme of neutral pastels, which move from grey tones at the entrance to white – the designer's favourite colour – in the cutting salons. The neutrality and purity of white, he says, is ideal for a minimalist project such as this one. Throughout the space, a play of shadows has been obtained with the use of industrial-style illumination supplied by Endo Lighting. One may ask how this pristine and highly refined space is able to function as a hair salon. After all, the processes that go into cutting, styling and colouring hair are messy, to say the least. Staff members, however, are conscious of the importance of keeping the place fastidiously clean and spotless, and the industrial paint used to finish the concrete floor remains unaffected by the 'hospital-style' scrubbing that follows each visit.

In explaining that this LIM interior is entirely in keeping with the philosophy of Isolation Unit, Yanagihara says that what he and his team do is 'more than just creating a product or interior'. Each commission 'develops from a simple view that circumstances surrounding the work being carried out within the space we are creating are important elements of the design'.

↑ Treatment commences on this stylish hair-washing lounger.

→ A wooden bookcase and chairs welcome guests between treatments.

↑ Graphic shapes and shadows
enliven the corridor.

↖ At LIM Hair Clinie, the reception
area is stark and mysterious.

↑ Low partition walls provide privacy while giving stylists an overall view of the salon interior.

← Before entering the salon, visitors leave all possessions at the reception desk.

architect

Isolation Unit
Teruhiro Yanagihara
Takagi Bld.3F,
Kyomachibori Nishiku
550-0003 Osaka
Japan
T +81 6 6459 1658
F +81 6 6459 2070
info@isolationunit.info
www.isolationunit.info

photographer

Takumi Ota
ota@phota.jp
www.phota.jp

legend

01 Reception
02 Shampoo box
03 Cutting and styling box
04 Staff room
05 Lavatories

0   3M

client
Toko
consultants
Takara Belmont and
Aveda Japan
manufacturer
Ishimaru
capacity
14 clients
total floor area (m²)
250

**duration of
construction**
2 months
opening
November 2006

project
Asta Aveda
1-1-3 Enoki,
Musashi-murayama
Tokyo 208-0022
Japan
T +81 42 562 5168
F +81 42 562 5169
mu@asta-aveda.com
www.asta-aveda.com

gps
N 25°2' E 121°27'

Curiosity
Asta Aveda
tokyo/japan

Text by Masaaki Takahashi

The minimalist design of the Asta Aveda Salon in Tokyo takes visitors on a woodland walk featuring artistic harmony, intriguing contrasts and an abundance of space. The range of elements and objects that result in a functional, relaxing interior also facilitate the smooth flow of people through the salon.

Aveda, a name synonymous with beauty products made from natural ingredients, is a comprehensive American cosmetics brand whose mission is to care for the world by doing business in a way that protects the earth.
The Asta Aveda Salon in Tokyo is a logical extension of the corporate philosophy. Aveda has a network of salons, spas, institutes and experience centres that spans the entire world. The brand can be proud of its latest addition. The Asta Aveda Salon is the work of Gwenael Nicholas, president of Tokyo-based design firm Curiosity. 'If Asta Aveda's "naturalness" concept – the idea of placing value on the customer – were to be expressed directly, without further refinement,' says Nicholas, 'it would fall short.' Nicholas's design sets itself apart by its striking simplicity. Rather than cluttering the interior, filling it to the brim or adorning it with superfluous objects, Nicholas chose to emphasize the relatively high ceilings and serene sightlines of the salon, using a strictly limited palette of materials and colours. The result is a space that features lucid volumes in largely blocky shapes, with a strong focus on artistic composition and the integration of architectural concepts. A major theme of the design is 'zero gravity' – a perfect description of the uncanny floating feeling conveyed by forms, lines and angles that make one wonder whether the floor and the ceiling

have changed places. The interior is composed of three main elements: water, stone and wood. The first is represented by surfaces of glass, the second by concrete flooring and the third by furnishings and wall panelling. Breaking the solidity of wood and stone – here in the form of concrete – is the subtle transparent quality of reflections softly pooling in glazed surfaces. At Asta Aveda, glass – with its ability to mirror its surroundings – has been used to express the contrasting and unpredictable forces of nature.
Located in a large suburban shopping mall in the district of Shibuya, the chic salon boasts a ceiling height of 4 metres. Nicholas's design accentuates this height, but not in an overwhelming way. Each of the salon's cocoon-like spaces provides a soothing haven of relaxation for Asta Aveda's clientele. 'In developing this design, I tried to recreate the feeling of walking in a forest, surrounded by towering trees,' is the designer's cryptic reference to the unique visual experience that emerges from a slow and sensory tour of the salon, with stops at every point of interest – and there are many.
Can we imagine ourselves in a forest, moving through an evolving though imperceptibly changing natural environment? Passing seamlessly through one area after another, as a smoothly progressing path takes us along

Indirect lighting creates a peaceful atmosphere, while adding a look of softness to surface materials.

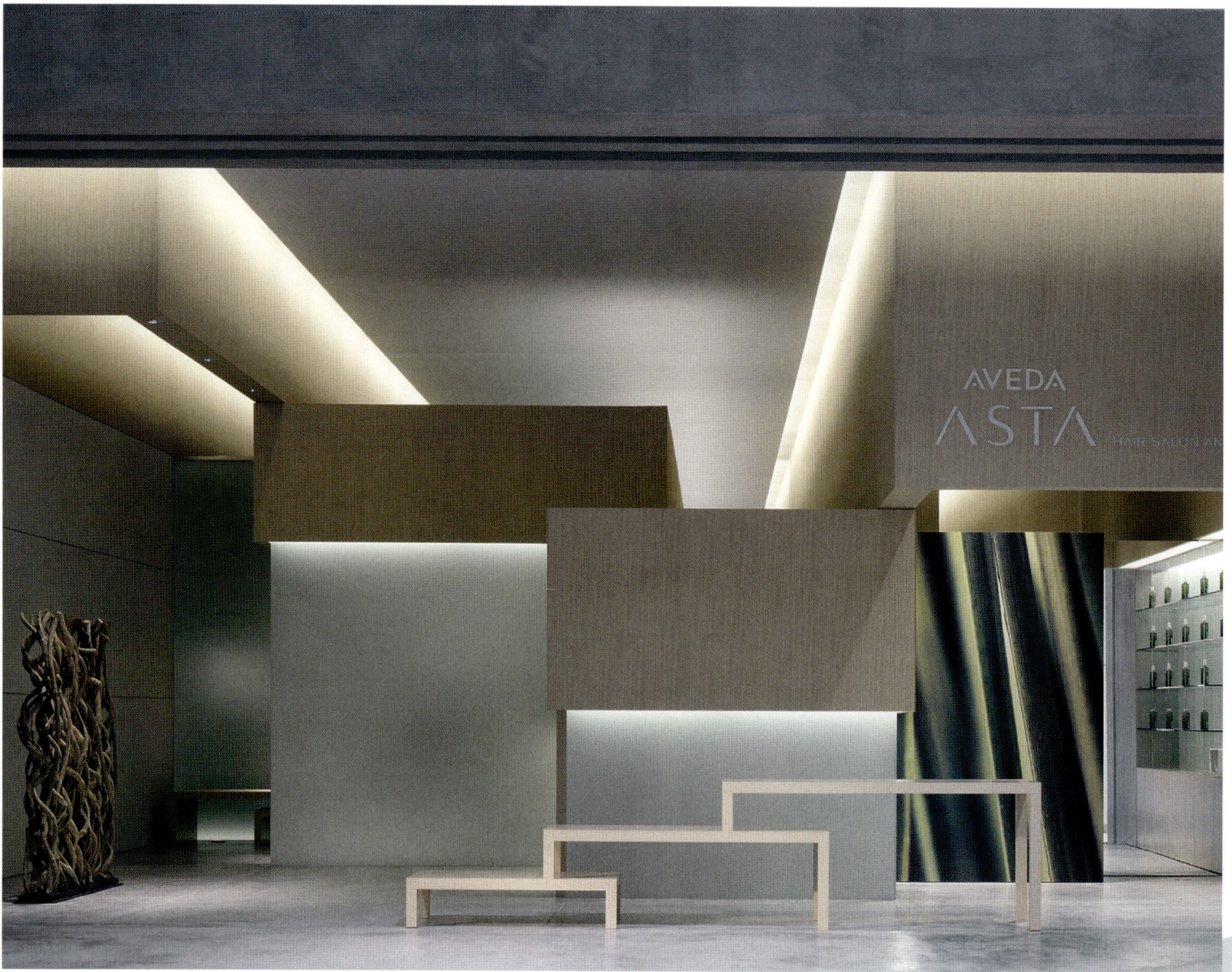

oak panels covering steel-and-plaster, ceiling-mounted volumes? Do we recognize areas physically linked to one another yet divided by function – a strategy that facilitates circulation within the salon? Overlapping oak panels form layers, while also generating a tangible rhythm that captures the eye. Here, Gwenael Nicholas has not simply produced an interior that reflects his thoughts; he's also taken into account the functional needs of a space dedicated to supplying a pampered elite with the ultimate in beauty treatments. Everywhere you look, you find evidence of an interior design aimed at affording a sense of comfort.

Drawn into the salon by an intriguing work of art near the entrance, the visitor finds herself standing in a simple reception area where a member of the Aveda staff stands behind a counter. Frosted glass – used extensively – reveals the faint shadows of those within. A large display wall presents the Aveda product line. Farther into the salon, two waiting areas furnished with seating radiate an aura of tranquillity; linking these areas is a stair-step configured set of display tables.

Passing the locker room, the client arrives at the hair-styling area, where tall mirrors again reinforce the height of the interior, create a sense of spaciousness and avoid isolating this section of the salon from the rest. Nicholas

designed the chairs in this area – arranged in a row of seven – to harmonize with their surroundings. Lining one side of the shampoo area, where a lowered ceiling is partially responsible for the calming atmosphere, are head spas that go with another seven comfortable chairs. These fully reclining loungers invite patrons to lie back and relax while having their hair washed.

Frosted glass is used effectively to give the impression of natural light, although most of the illumination is the result of artificial, indirect lighting, which plays across all the salon's larger surfaces. Good use has been made of reflection, textures and materials, namely wood and glass, the latter of which lends a soft transparency to the entire salon. Asta Aveda is sure to have an impact on those looking for a place that radiates the kind of beauty they hope to find for themselves.

↑ The rhythmic design of the façade ushers passers-by into the salon.

→ Angular volumes, concrete flooring and a dropped ceiling create a dynamic backdrop that stimulates visitors to move through the interior.

Boxes and bottles from Bali lend
a touch of the exotic to the Asta
Aveda Salon.

Natural materials used throughout this minimalist interior bear no trace of clichéd Japanese styles.

The interior is composed of three main elements: *water, stone and wood* – represented by glass, concrete and panelling, respectively

↑ Seven custom-made chairs form a row beneath the dropped ceiling.

→ Gwenael Nicholas of Curiosity used natural materials and configured furniture and design elements to evoke the sense of a woodland setting.

architect

Curiosity
Gwenael Nicolas
2-13-16 Tomigaya,
Shibuya-ku
Tokyo 151-0063
Japan
T +81 3 5452 0095
F +81 3 5454 9691
info@curiosity.jp
www.curiosity.jp

photographer

Nacása & Partners
shooting@nacasa.co.jp
www.nacasa.co.jp/e/

legend
01 Locker room
02 Counselling room
03 Shampoo area
04 Cutting area
05 Head spas
06 Relaxation area
07 Laboratory
08 Rest rooms

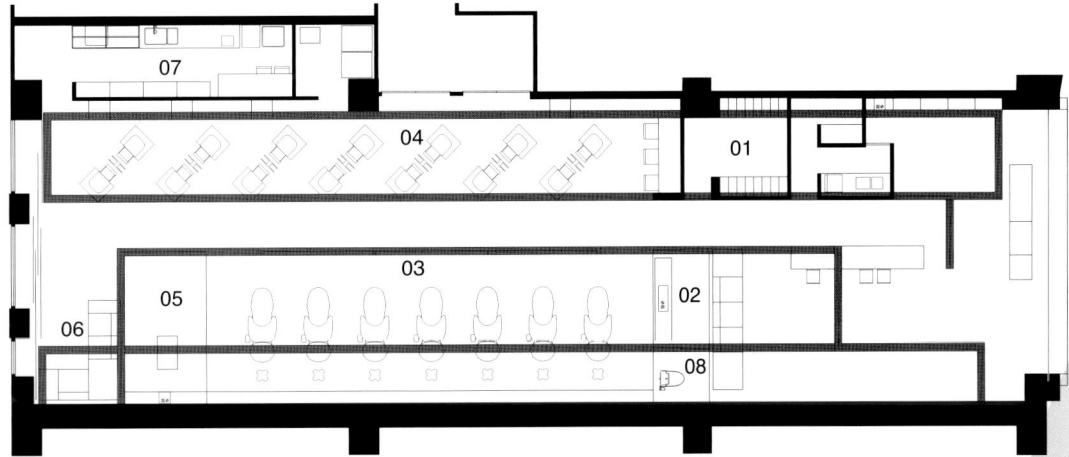

Karim Rashid
Retail Concept

Text by Tim Groen

Asked to develop a retail concept that would work equally well in a department store and in an independent location on a busy shopping street, Karim Rashid came up with a versatile space defined by curvy wood surfaces and a predominance of freestanding furniture.

In 2003 an international fashion brand asked Karim Rashid to create a retail concept for its new cosmetics line. Because the client intended to roll out a chain of boutiques in cities all over the world, it was crucial that Karim's concept not be limited by location. 'The only thing one keeps in mind is that generally most stores in urban centres are similar,' says Karim. 'I tried to design for the typical proportions of a shop, so that when the actual project locations were found, the concept and feeling would still work.'

The line of make-up and skincare products includes five looks and skin types. Basing his plan on a 200-m^2 space – a size thought to represent the average location – the designer developed a store around five service islands floating in a sea of wood. He kept these stations, with their glossy black-and-white finishes, simple and clean to contrast with curved wood-veneered walls and ceilings and hardwood floors. Each modular station provides an appropriate seating area for one-on-one attention. Translating Karim's retail concept to smaller spaces necessitated a modular approach comprising mass-produced display units and furnishings. Having entered the retail space, the customer has three choices: to take an 'educational' tour of the collection at a product counter or at a Distinctive Look technology wall; to work with a consultant at a centrally located application station; or, if she already knows what she wants, to proceed to the rear service counter to make her purchase. The project gave

Karim a chance to source a range of new technologies, including digital cameras and sensors, mirrors backed with LCD monitors, colour-correcting light, and computerized skin-sensor programs. 'The idea is a super high-tech health and beauty experience, and the greatest part of the design, for me, was finding new technologies with which to create an experiential place – something that goes beyond what exists already in the world of cosmetics and that embraces the digital age.'

Entrance doors are part of a wall of tinted glass. Two doors on either side of the centre panel slide open and closed, creating colours where they overlap: tints in blushing pinks and rosy beiges. This feature suggests the blending of cosmetic colours to create that very special look. Flanking the glass doors are two round display windows framed in mirrored chrome: ellipsoid spheres reflecting the street and the window-shopper.

To avoid alienating shoppers with an overdose of high tech, the designer warmed the space with the organic curves of wood walls and ceiling, inspired by the hull of an exotic yacht. 'I don't like walls or boundaries,' says Karim, who believes that the delineation of boxy spaces makes for a restrictive and claustrophobic interior.

Glossy black shelving flows along the length of the space and meets at a rear counter which is set against a wall of blue mirrored chrome, an element selected to represent brand identity: in this case, a fusion of classic, modern and sporty. The glossy finish of certain furnishings ties in to

Specifically designed to flatter the skin of customers experimenting with beauty products is a compound curved ceiling equipped with LED cove lighting.

← The introduction of the brand starts with the façade, where sliding doors made of tinted glass suggest the blending of make-up colours.

the look of the packaging. Running down the middle of the space are three grooves of light aglow with the warm colours of the product line. The central islands are also surrounded by light wells, which illuminate the faces of these modular units, reflecting the mood of the line and thus the ambience generated by Karim's retail concept. The project remained a concept, but Karim has since created projects that not only expand on the high-tech aspects of this retail design, but on its global marketing objectives as well. 'I'm a big believer in the borderless age, where location should not matter,' he says. 'Globalization is creating one world, seamless and free.'

> ## 'I'm a big believer in the *borderless age*, where location should not matter; globalization is creating one world, seamless and free'
> «Karim Rashid»

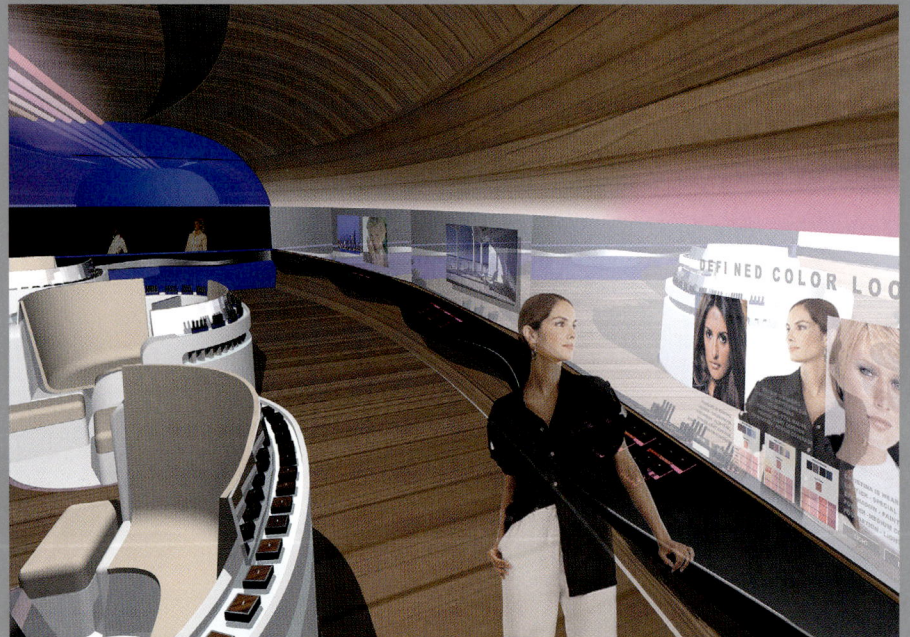

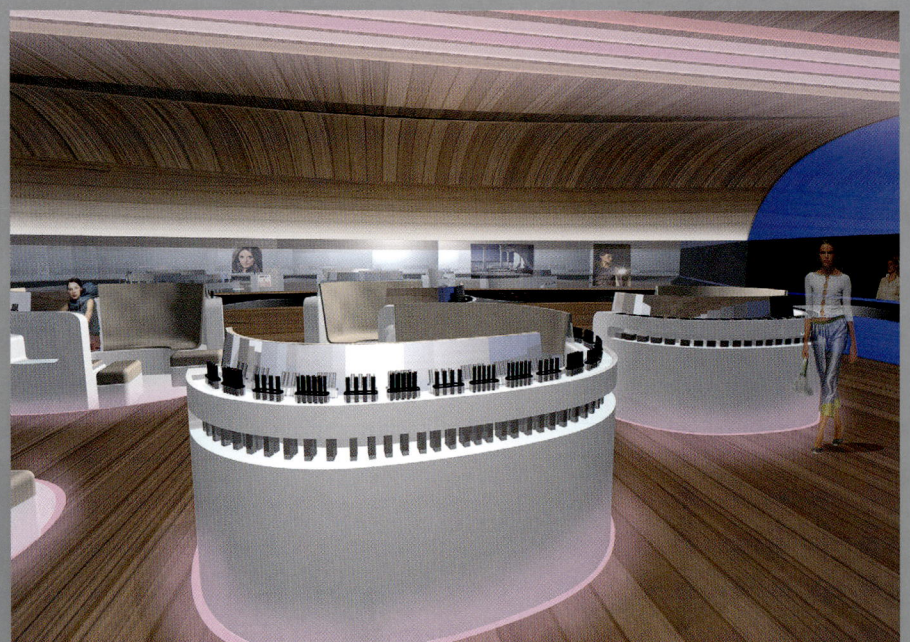

architect
Karim Rashid
357 West 17th Street
New York, NY 10011
USA
T +1 212 929 8657
F +1 212 929 0247
office@karimrashid.com
www.karimrashid.com

legend
01 Lipstick counter
02 Application station
03 Product display
04 Cashier and service counter

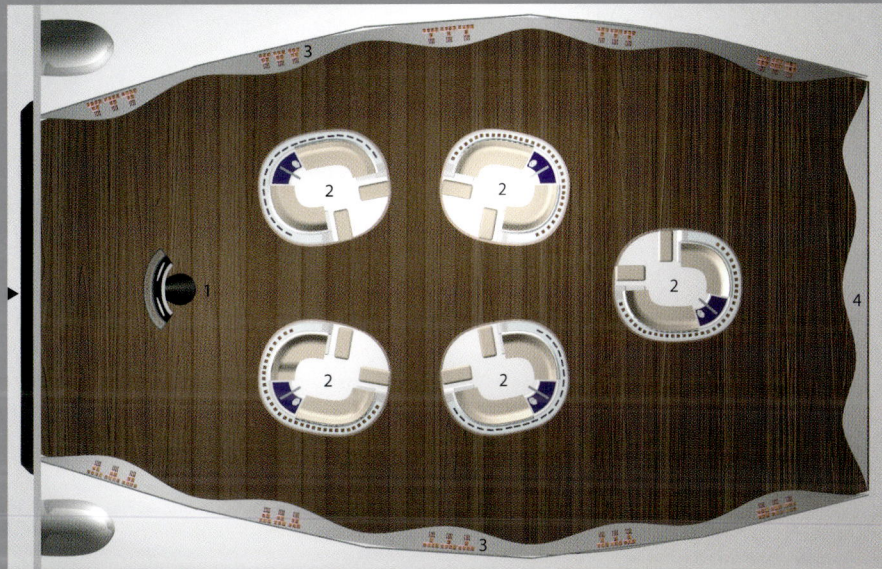

↖ A high-tech experience: walls clad in wood veneer are combined with surfaces of laminated coloured glass and LCD monitors.

↖ Karim Rashid, who feels that most boxy spaces are claustrophobic, suggested the sort of organic flow that gives the hull of a yacht its streamlined look.

← Forming the core of the space are modular service islands that provide customers and sales personnel with ample space for one-on-one consultations. The stations feature a neutral palette, which is complemented by a glossy exterior finish that echoes product packaging.

Section 03

Gyms

Text by Karim Rashid
'Let's get physical'
Olivia Newton John, 1984

The commonality shared by all diets is the need for physical fitness. Essential to our wellbeing, physical fitness helps fend off disease, keeps us looking younger, de-stresses the body and enriches our lives on every level. Just as we need to exercise the brain, we need to exercise the body, and today's gym can attest to both. The gym has changed drastically since I started going in the '70s. Prior to the '70s gyms were virtually inhuman, not a public destination or activity – they tended to be specialized locations for bodybuilders and weightlifters (generally devoid of women), boxing clubs, or places exclusively for gymnastics.

In the '70s, however, the gym became the daytime disco: a unisex spot for socializing and a venue where diverse physical activities took place. By the '80s, the gym had become a social piazza, complete with shiny Lycra and headbands à la Jane Fonda. But, honestly, the gym has not changed drastically. Gyms tend to be barren, noncommittal, warehouse-like spaces containing lots of equipment and aerobics rooms with wood floors. The major change in gyms has been the equipment. Equipment has increased tenfold in technology. Gym machines have become very sophisticated – I'm presently designing several hotels with gyms, and I am specifying gym equipment that was unheard of only ten years ago: treadmills that are like running on air, that read your pulse via your feet, that house flat-screen touch-sensitive monitors and have built-in fans that blow cool air. Weightlifting machines have more sophisticated, balanced actions that target muscles better without

putting strain on other parts of your body; more comfortable, smoother interfaces; digital feedback and so forth. Even dumbbells are more pleasant to grab, more colourful, more ergonomic. Recycled-rubber floors, acoustic considerations, large graphics and imagery, and other improvements in the gym have evolved over time. I work out in gyms all over the world but still see very little colour or anything unusual, inspiring or provoking. There is a lack of colour and design that should stimulate and imbue energy and positive thinking. Gyms have diversified in their activities and include climbing walls, spinning rooms, yoga rooms and Pilates machines. A plethora of new directions in fitness techniques are forever being invented, but often the gym itself is uneventful. The gym will eventually transcend into a place that raises the spirit and conveys a feeling of health and fitness. The selected projects on the following pages show this ongoing transformation.

'Prior to the '70s gyms were *virtually inhuman*, not a public destination or activity' «Karim»

client
Yoga Plus
engineer
Far East Consulting
Engineers
manufacturer
Pakee Decoration

graphic design
Cream
total floor area (m²)
1500
opening
October 2005

project
Yoga Plus
5-7/F, LKF Tower
33 Wyndham Street
Central, Hong Kong
China
T +852 2901 2901
F +852 2901 2900
info@yogaplus.com.hk
www.yogaplus.com.hk

gps
N 22°18' E 114°10'

Cream
Yoga Plus
hong kong/china

Text by Masaaki Takahashi

As yoga gains in popularity across the globe, local designers asked to craft facilities for yoga often forge environments that complement specific regional cultures. The attractive interior at Yoga Plus, however, is grounded in a universal language that goes beyond physical exercise to heal both body and mind.

Hong Kong's vibrant Lan Kwai Fong district is one of the cosmopolitan island's more lively destinations. As you stroll along avenues thronged with pleasure seekers, you find yourself surrounded by the sound of English tinged with a rich diversity of accents. Here the streets are lined with cafés and restaurants featuring culinary delights from all over the world. Popular among Westerners residing in Hong Kong, Lan Kwai Fong is known primarily as a stylish entertainment area with a varied range of nightlife. Tucked away within this busy district, however, is a sanctuary of calm: Yoga Plus. This yoga and Pilates studio can be found in Lan Kwai Fong's LKF Tower, a development renowned for its emphasis on quality design. Commanding a view of the bustling streets below, Yoga Plus occupies the fifth, sixth and seventh floors of the high rise: three levels that contain a total floor area of 1500 m². Health-care and relaxation facilities such as spas and yoga studios now play an important role in attracting guests to hotels in metropolises throughout the world, and luxury hotels in Hong Kong are no exception. Hoteliers introduce an array of cutting-edge facilities and design in their efforts to appeal to potential clients. The look for Yoga Plus was created by designer Antony Chan, who heads up local interior-design firm Cream, an outfit that has built

a strong reputation based on plush residential interiors. Chan not only took responsibility for the interior, but also designed stationery and signage for Yoga Plus, as well as a corporate identity. His in-depth research for this project included visits to existing yoga studios in the city – all part of his quest to produce something out of the ordinary. Opting to go beyond mere glitz and opulence for effect, Chan focused on sensuous, quality materials and a serene atmosphere to achieve his delightful and incredibly stylish interior.

The main, sixth-floor reception area is a blend of sandstone and grey granite. Visitors stepping out of the lift are welcomed by staff stationed at a long, translucent counter backed by vertical bands in lime green, the corporate colour and a fresh note that enlivens the soothing ambience. Patrons remove their shoes and slip into comfortable 'shoe socks' before moving farther into the space. The sixth floor is what the designer has dubbed the 'fun zone.' It houses a yoga and dance studio, men's and women's changing rooms, a yoga pro shop and a juice bar. The combination of amenities results in a space that quietly encourages all who enter to relax.

Wooden surfaces on changing-room lockers lend additional warmth to the space, while a luxurious,

Playful references to the
Cream-designed logo appear in
various perforated wall panels
and etched wall treatments.

multi-hued Italian mosaic floor and textured walls above the benches instantly influence the guest's state of mind, drawing each potential yogi away from the frenetic workaday world outside. It's an oasis of warm, sedative tones; walls lined in thin vertical bands of oak; and floors of creamy sandstone. Delicately strewn across the walnut feature wall are the curves and cutouts of the company motif, a flower with four petals that enhances the striking look of the lounge. Vertical slats dip and swoop on ceiling surfaces, adding a playful touch to the interior. Ascending to the seventh floor, patrons find themselves in the spa zone, which features a members-only spa, six massage rooms (two of which contain twin massage tables), a cosy relaxation area that can accommodate up to five people, changing rooms and a sauna. Two levels down, the fifth floor is divided into a spacious mirrored studio, a meeting room and three instruction rooms for private classes, each with a floor area of between 60 and 90 m². This level of the facility also boasts an advanced Pilates and Gyrotonics studio that is kitted out with training equipment made in America, such as a Pilates Trapeze Table, a Pilates Ladder Barrel, a Revo Footbar and a Gyrotonics Pulley Tower.

Chan wanted to express the themes of health, fun and harmony throughout his interior: one aspect that reveals

his attention to detail is the way in which he has meticulously designed the three floors to make guests experience a sense of lightness and tranquillity that intensifies with each ascending level.

The majority of the Yoga Plus instructors are natives of India who have received specialist training and certification in their fields of expertise. They offer a variety of classes, including one for golfers! The popularity of the studio is growing fast; the concept may even develop into a chain, in which case we'll see Yoga Plus studios opening in other Asian cities.

↑ Mirrored walls and a range of high-tech exercise equipment in the Pilates and Gyrotonics studio push users of this state-of-the-art space to reach their full potential.

→ Light passing through this sandblasted glass wall, a surface composed of overlapping layers with a floral motif, bathes the changing-room foyer in a soothing flow of illumination.

Treatment rooms combine wood surfaces and sophisticatedly clean-cut forms to establish a contemporary but lavish atmosphere.

Mosaic, marble and wood are the key materials of the changing room, where even the ceiling makes a sculptural statement.

← The signature motif –
a stylized flower with four
petals – is repeated throughout
the studio.

↑ Visitors entering the reception
area, with its long translucent
counter, see a textured stone
wall bearing the Cream-
designed logo.

Patrons remove their
shoes and slip into
comfortable *'shoe socks'*
before moving farther
into the space

architect

Cream
2203 Lyndhurst Tower
1 Lyndhurst Terrace
Central, Hong Kong
China
T +852 2147 1297
F +852 2147 0118
info@cream.com.hk
www.cream.com.hk

photographer

Virgile Simon Bertrand
info@red-desert.com.hk
www.red-desert.com.hk

legend
01 Reception
02 Lockers
03 Lounge
04 Shop
05 Juice bar
06 Changing room
07 Dance and yoga studio
08 Gym
09 Private classroom
10 Massage room
11 Sauna
12 Relaxation room
13 Staff room
14 Meeting room
15 Storage

Seventh floor

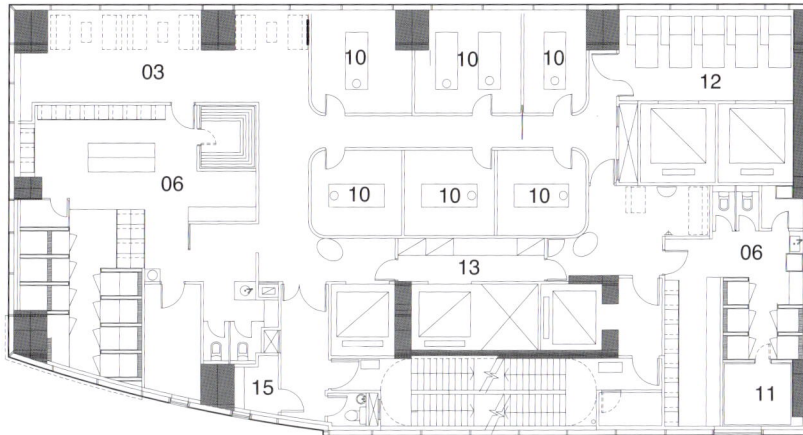

Sixth floor

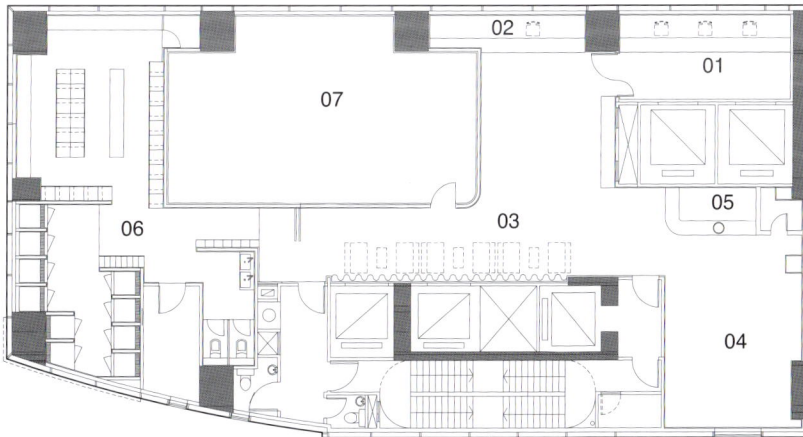

Fifth floor

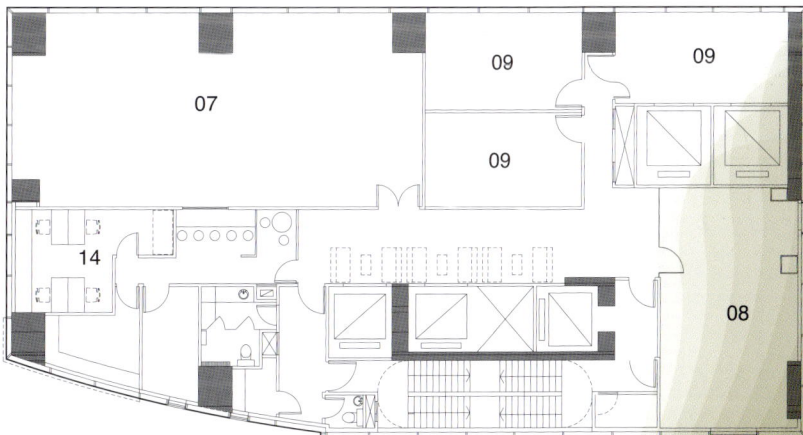

client
Pusteblume Zentrum
engineer
Franken & Kreft
manufacturers
Sto, Freudenberg, Royal
Mosa, Villeroy & Boch,
Drapilux, Recycled,
RZB, Ansorg, Jung,
FSB, Duravit, Keramag,
Grohe, Franke, Benz and
Berlintapete

**custom-made
furniture**
Jugendhilfe Cologne
and Meta
graphic design
ideengestalt
total floor area (m²)
150
**duration of
construction**
4 months

opening
May 2006
project
Pusteblume Centre
Ansgarplatz
50825 Cologne
Germany
T +49 221 9559 377
info@pusteblume-online.de
www.pusteblume-online.de

gps
N 50°57' E 006°55'

100% interior
Pusteblume

cologne/germany

Text by Anneke Bokern

Spherical lamps, juicy colour contrasts and photos of ordinary people characterize the Pusteblume Centre for dance, gymnastics and leisure activities. Space was limited, but Sylvia Leydecker of 100% interior used the simplest of means to create an interior that is both minimalist and highly playful.

A gap-toothed girl with freckles and blonde plaits greets visitors to the Pusteblume Centre in Cologne. The natural glow of her cheeky grin radiates from a large photo on a wall by the stairwell. Sylvia Leydecker of Cologne-based 100% interior explains: 'Her name is Lulu, and we found her among our own circle of friends and acquaintances. Rather than a groomed child model, we wanted to use an ordinary kid who looks as though she's just returned from the playground. I even made sure that her hair wasn't combed for the photo.'

'Normality' and 'bright colours' are keywords describing Leydecker's design for Pusteblume. Backing the smiling Lulu is a raspberry-red wall flanked on either side by a grass-green wall – a vivid scene underlined by a floor of cornflower blue. A striking combination, indeed, but one that is nonetheless easy on the eye. It all comes down to Leydecker's skilful selection of hues.

'I met Pusteblume's director at a cultural exchange,' Leydecker says, 'and we clicked immediately. He told me he'd soon be opening a second centre. When he contacted me a few weeks later, he asked me to design the new spaces. He was afraid we would be way beyond his budget, but I regarded his limited budget as a challenge. It's all too easy to be expensive.'

With minimal means, Leydecker transformed the 150-m² ground floor and basement of an old parish library into a studio for dance, gymnastics and leisure activities. Unlike most commercial fitness studios, Pusteblume, which originally sprang from a communal initiative, does not target the rich and the beautiful. 'People who come here are completely average and include children, singles and older clients. The image is bright, cheerful and, above all, unusually ordinary,' says Leydecker, who is surely aware that her statement is paradoxical.

All corridors at the centre are bright. According to Leydecker, the colours are consistent with the corporate identity of Pusteblume. 'We've just given them a slight update. Right from the start, they were part of the overall design concept. My client wanted Pusteblume to be a unique and unforgettable experience with a great feel-good factor. Despite spatial restrictions, we achieved his goal mainly through colour effects, which structure the various areas. No one who has visited Pusteblume will ever forget it.'

In the dance studio, where classes take place and where pupils and teachers spend a great deal of time, colours are more placid and more natural. Warm shades of brown and beige predominate, the ceiling is wood panelled,

'The image is bright, cheerful and, above all, *unusually ordinary*'

«Sylvia Leydecker»

UMKLEIDE

← The colour scheme of each room is repeated in the signage used to guide visitors to the various areas of the centre.

↑ Changing rooms are dominated by cornflower-blue walls and simple furniture.

translucent curtains in front of the mirrors can be drawn shut to conceal cellulite exercising. An 8-m long side wall features a hazy print of dandelion clocks – called *Pusteblumen* or 'blow flowers' in German.

The only splashes of colour are a few bright-blue gym balls incorporated into another wall as pieces of functional equipment that also add a decorative touch to the room. 'One problem was that we didn't know where to put the gym equipment in such a confined space. We could stow most things in a wall cupboard or in movable chests. But large balls take up a lot of space. So I decided to put them on display,' says Leydecker. Her decision gave birth to the spherical motif that went on to permeate the centre. Epoxy-resin floors in blue and green, for example, are covered with tiny glass balls called *ballotini*, and various sizes of round paper lamps hang in groups throughout the interior.

Besides these incredibly inexpensive lamps, Leydecker relied on tubular lighting for the corridors and reused lamps from the old library in the rest of the centre. There is not a trace of designer furniture at Pusteblume. All furniture was made by members of a youth project in Cologne.

Chic designer furniture would hardly have fitted with the concept of 'normality'. Lulu would smear every seat and backrest with her chocolaty fingers. And the older ladies, looking out from a tiled frieze in the changing area, would not have known what to make of it. 'We simply selected old photos taken in Pusteblume classes and had them transferred to tiles. These are just ordinary elderly women. Whatever else, I didn't want them to look like an advertising brochure for an exclusive retirement home,' says the designer. The result of all her efforts is an impressive interior that skilfully avoids any kind of commerciality, while never sacrificing the standards that Leydecker applies to her work.

Looking like a cheeky kid sister of Pippi Longstocking, Lulu grins from the wall. She's part of a concept that embraces the enjoyment of ordinary things.

The large gymnasium
features warm shades of
brown and beige.

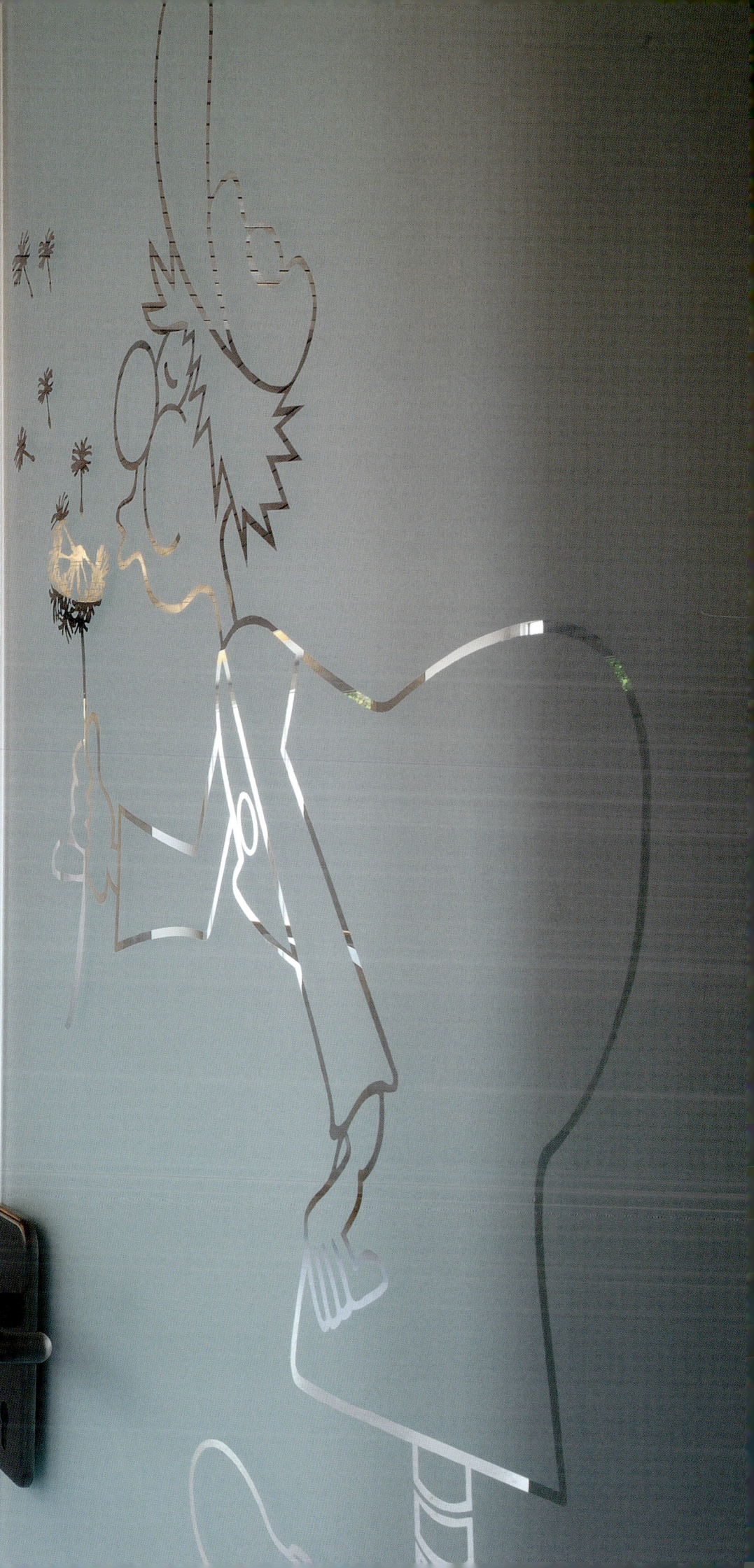

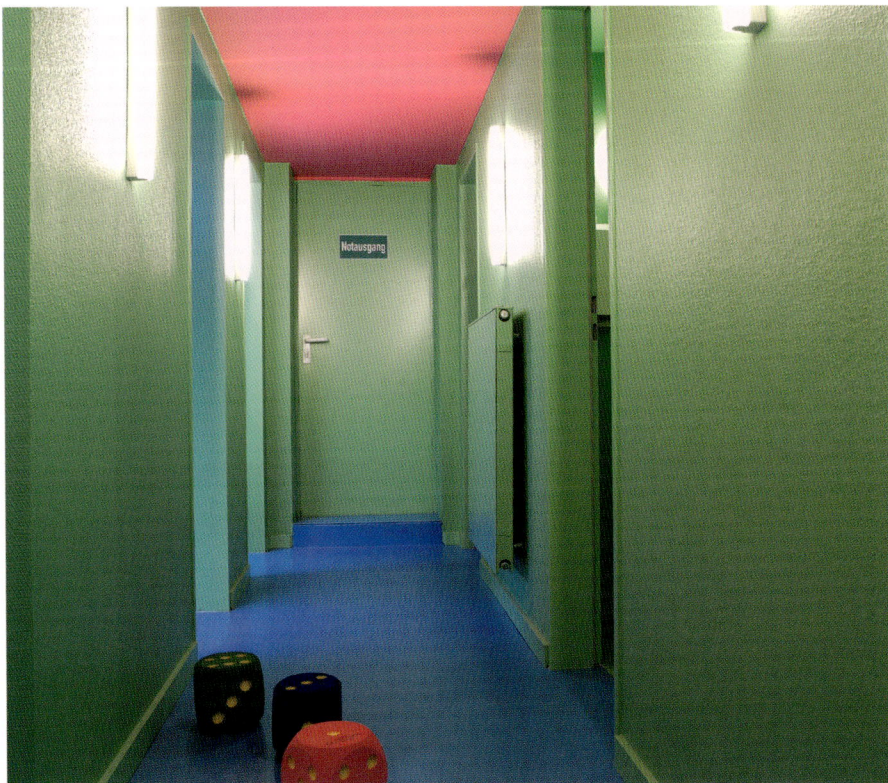

architect
100% interior,
Sylvia Leydecker
Johannes-Mueller-Str. 25
50735 Cologne
Germany
T +49 221 7363 83
interior@netcologne.de
www.100interior.de

photographer
Karin Hessmann
fotodesign@
karin-hessmann.de
www.karin-hessmann.de

legend
01 Changing room
02 Waiting area
03 Dance room
04 Play room
05 Hall
06 Lavatories
07 Storage

Ground floor

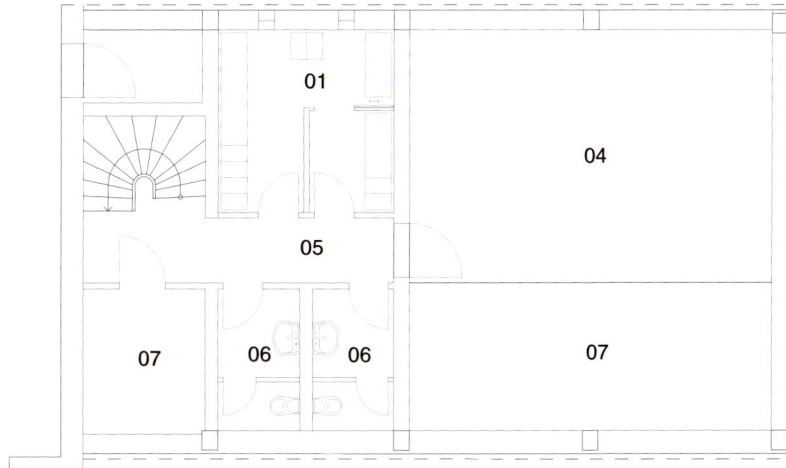

Basement

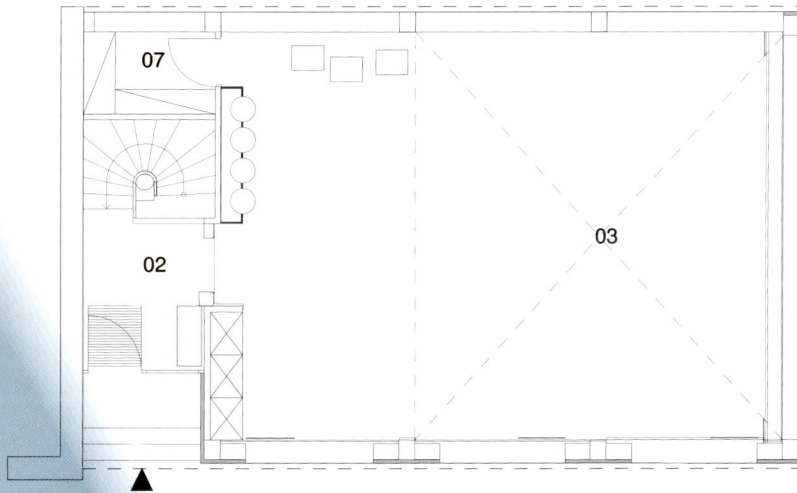

↖ The designers' creative use of
space includes brightly coloured
gym balls that double as
sculptural wall elements.

← Pink ceiling, green walls and
a blue floor create an ensemble
that visitors are sure to
remember.

← Grass-green rules. Rest rooms
are no less colourful than the
other spaces at Pusteblume.

client
Physical STN
manufacturers
Ebisu textile art:
Asami Kiyokawa
Omotesando climbing wall:
Hotch Hold and Board
capacity
Ebisu: 150 clients
Omotesando: 150 clients
total floor area (m²)
Ebisu: 660
Omotesando: 850

total cost (€)
Ebisu: 642,000
Omotesando: 734,000
**duration of
construction**
Ebisu: 2 months
Omotesando: 2 months
opening
Ebisu: October 2006
Omotesando: December
2006

project
Illoiha Ebisu
4-3-1-3F Ebisu, Shibuya-ku
Tokyo 150-0013
Japan
-
Illoiha Omotesando
3-5-12-B1F, B2F Kita-
Aoyama, Minato-ku
Tokyo 107-0061
Japan

gps
N 35°40' E 139°45'

Nendo
Illoiha Ebisu and Omotesando
tokyo/japan

Text by Masaaki Takahashi

A matched pair of fitness clubs in Tokyo offer patrons visually stimulating features such as an eye-catching fabric on the ceiling and a custom-made series of humorous grips on a climbing wall. Cool interiors and design that speaks a thousand words set these clubs apart from conventional gyms.

With a portfolio that ranges from chewing-gum packaging and corporate logos to interiors and architecture, design firm Nendo is well placed to create a look for almost any client that comes its way. In 2006, Physical STN invited the firm to put together an interior for its latest project, a matched pair of designer fitness clubs for urbanites. Located in two of Tokyo's more stylish areas, the gyms share a name – Illoiha – conceived by Nendo's CEO, Oki Sato. Although the name has a slight Hawaiian ring to it and a pronunciation similar to LOHAS (a marketing acronym for 'lifestyles of health and sustainability'), Sato says it refers to phi or the golden section (1:1.618), revered for centuries by artists, architects and mathematicians for its unique aesthetic qualities. Illoiha is a homonym. Correctly pronounced, it sounds very much like the digits of the golden section as they are pronounced in Japanese. In line with their distinctive name, the fitness clubs share the concept of an ideal body balance combined with an aesthetic appeal. The brand's décor features gold as its key colour, while the golden section was also used as the basis for all graphics. In addition, the designers

created a brand mascot whose head is made from a golden rectangle, an impressive character that appears in various places throughout the premises. The use of a trademark creature of this kind is a device regularly used in Japan to familiarize users with a brand image.
The Ebisu branch of Illoiha – the complex is right next to Ebisu Station – offers a wide variety of programmes that target the club's predominantly female clientele. Activities include yoga lessons, lava baths and fitness classes. With the programmes and the clientele in mind, Sato used the interior design to express what he calls 'a sensitivity to and an awareness of the beauty-enhancing potential of physical movement'.
The most eye-catching element at Illoiha Ebisu is surely the ceiling of the 50-m-long passageway, which forms the main line of circulation through the gym. Enclosed beneath a layer of glass is a stunning swathe of fabric designed by textile artist Asami Kiyokawa. Stitched together from lengths of handmade organdie, lace and synthetic material, the piece was placed behind glass that was then covered with a sheet of view-control film.

Omotesando: Targeting
Illoiha's female clientele is an
undulating white climbing wall
with a surprisingly amusing
array of grips.

When looked at straight on, the fabric beneath the film is clearly visible. From an angle, however, the film becomes semi-opaque, acting to conceal what lies beneath. The unique characteristics of the film encourage visitors to keep moving in an effort to get the ceiling to reveal its secrets. Their movement is rewarded with the opportunity to appreciate the true beauty of the fabric. Of special interest is Nendo's use of this visual device in a way that is diametrically opposed to the conventional purpose of the material, which is to conceal something that is not meant to be seen. Here, the film has been applied to a glazed surface to draw attention to a key element of the design. The second Illoiha branch is on Omotesando Boulevard in the neighbourhood of the same name. The gym occupies underground premises and covers two floors. In order to avoid a sense of claustrophobia, an unfortunate side effect of many basement locations, as well as to unify the space and create a smooth transition between floors, Sato focused attention on the void that connects the two levels. He made this zone the focal point of the project, using it to express the brand concept. The designer achieved his goal with the improbable introduction into the space of a double-height climbing wall. Spurning the straightforward grips usually found on such practice walls, he played with the conceptual mismatch between a rugged outdoor sport and the gym's location in fashionable Omotesando, moulding a fantastical array of picture frames, mirrors, deer heads, birdcages and vases – a mad medley of objects that he placed in intentionally challenging positions. 'I hope it gives people who are completely unfamiliar with rock climbing the desire to give the sport a try, and that it may even launch a new fitness style,' confides Sato.

The climbing wall was constructed out of fibre-reinforced plastic by an extremely experienced firm that specializes in developing and installing this type of equipment for sporting facilities. The gently undulating wall evokes an image of soft drapes hanging from the lofty ceiling, while the decorative objects attached to its surface emphasize a theme based on elements found in domestic interiors. Climbers have the choice of three routes to the top – separated by protruding 'waves' and mapped out in consultation with professional climbers – each representing a different level of difficulty. To add variety and cater to an even wider range of ability, grips can be removed from the wall and rearranged to create new routes.

'I hope the climbing wall gives people who are completely unfamiliar with rock climbing the desire to give the sport a try, and that it may even *launch a new fitness style*' «Oki Sato»

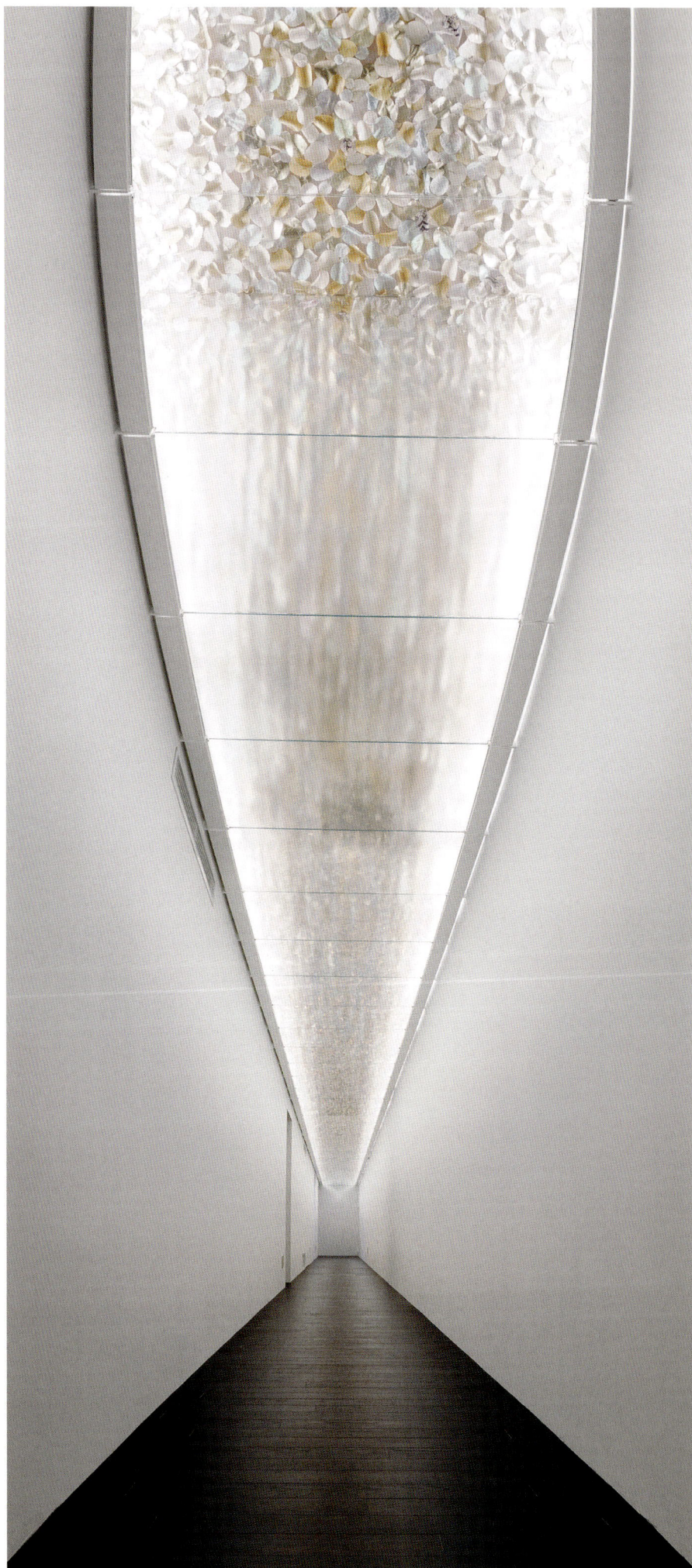

Ebisu: The unique ceiling of this 50-m-long hallway consists of a swathe of fabric behind glass that has been clad in a sheet of view control film. The pattern on the fabric changes when looked at from different angles.

ILLOIHA
FITNESS *1.618* RELAXATION

Omotesando: High-gloss paint
and bright lights visually open
up the space and prevent feelings
of claustrophobia.

↑ Ebisu: A yellow-and-gold colour scheme refers to the so-called 'golden section', which Nendo chose as the theme of its interior design.

← Ebisu: The gym occupies a basement location.

architect
Nendo
4-1-20-2A Mejiro,
Toshima-ku
Tokyo 171-0031
Japan
T +81 3 3954 5554
F +81 3 3954 5581
info@nendo.jp
www.nendo.jp

photographer
Daici Ano
ano@fwdinc.jp

legend
01 Reception
02 Lobby
03 Changing room
04 Counselling room
05 Sauna
06 Yoga Studio
07 Pilates room
08 Massage room
09 Gym
10 Climbing wall
11 Showers
12 Café
13 Kitchen
14 Staff room
15 Lavatories
16 Storage

Illoiha Ebisu

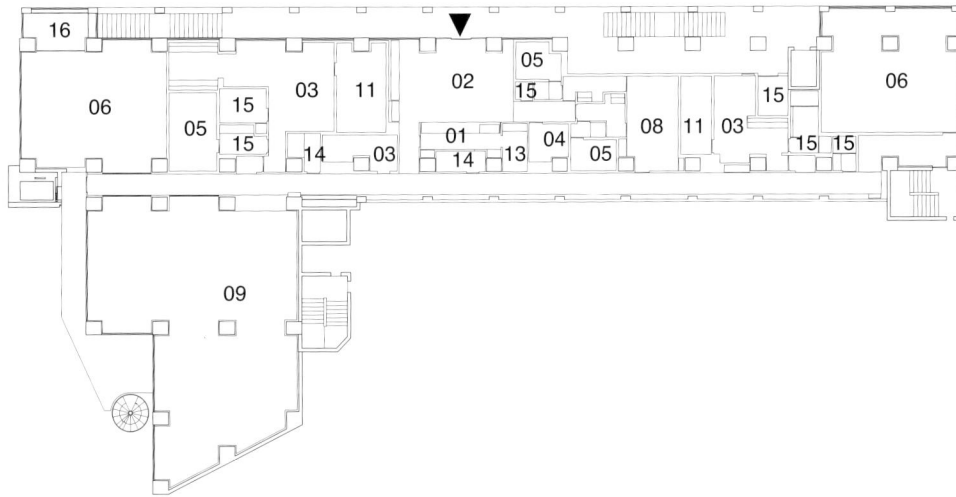

Illoiha Omotesando
First basement

Second basement

client
Dakis Joannou
consultants
Focus Lighting and
Fibrepro
architect of record
K. Kyriakidis & Associates
manufacturers
Artemide, Bizazza, Fasem,
Foscarini, Frighetto,
Galerkin, Gandia Blasco,
Idee, Kovacs/Minka
Group, Magis, Nambe,
Nienkamper, Pure Design,
Vidrepur, Umbra, Zeritalia
and Zerodisegno

total floor area (m²)
12,000
total cost ($)
22 million
budget per m² ($)
1820
**duration of
construction**
3 years
opening
2004

project
Semiramis Hotel
48 Charilaou Trikoupi Street
14562 Kifissia, Athens
Greece
T +30 210 628 4400
F +30 210 628 4499
info@semiramisathens.com
www.semiramisathens.com

gps
N 37°59' E 023°44'

Karim Rashid
Semiramis Hotel Spa, Gym and Pool
athens/greece

Text by Shonquis Moreno

Each year, Karim Rashid travels an average of 200 days, sleeps in over 100 hotel beds and jogs at least 2000 km on hotel treadmills. Cataloguing his grievances about the design and amenities of many of these swank lodgings, Karim concludes that 'hotels should be soft and human'. And he's set out to transform his wish into reality.

For Greek art collector Dakis Joannou, Karim gutted and redesigned a 1920s-era hotel 340 m above the Aegean Sea. The $22-million, 52-room Athens hotel seems to have popped from the designer's sherbet-coloured brain. Fraught with high-energy colour and soothing texture and embedded with technology, the Semiramis Hotel welcomes guests with sensors set every 15 cm throughout the corridors, which light up and fade in the wake of passers-by; coloured glass partitions that offer melting views through the interiors; and scrolling LED screens outside each room that guests can program with personal messages. Karim designed nearly everything: from an amoeboid pool to the towels, from restaurant matches to receptionists' pens, from pastel-coloured vials of mouthwash to staff uniforms. And with the aptly named

Karim – a shop at street level stocked with Karim Rashid watches, bed linens and lamps – the designer is out-W-ing the W and out-Starcking Ian Schrager. 'I want to climb the tower, to reach utopia,' Karim says. 'In the Semiramis, I have developed my own little utopia.'
All of a piece with Karim's utopia-building, the hotel's spa, gym and pool areas are based on the designer's on-the-go experiences and his relentless brand of positivism. At the Semiramis, areas of an architectural project traditionally reserved for the cultivation of wellbeing are not distinguished from other types of space. All parts of the hotel equally and emphatically focus on evoking health and pleasure. The spa does not follow the lead of its host, a particularly joyful pastel-tiled hotel; nor does the hotel takes its cue from the spa. Instead, the two

↑ Karim's hotel includes a discrete spa but tends not to distinguish the appearance of spaces devoted to wellbeing from any other type of space in the building, including hotel rooms and corridors.

← The hotel's swimming pool features a wood deck and Karim-designed lounge furniture.

are part and parcel of a single euphoric master plan.
From the dining room, glass doors lead directly onto a
voluptuously curved pool. 'I focused on marrying the
restaurant to the bar and the pool so that there was a flow,
an outwardness, a connection with the inner and the
outer, with technology, and nature,' Karim explains.
'I wanted it to have effulgence and yet be calming.'
An arcing deck with low, bright-white walls and five
bungalows collars the pool, which is tiled in soft, lucid
hues. 'The Semiramis could exist anywhere in the world
and, at the same time, only in Athens,' the designer
insists. 'This is because it was influenced by the local
environment: the choice of materials, the pool shaped
like a Greek island, the topography of the region.
The colours were inspired by the sunsets here – the pinks,
the yellows, the beauty of the amazing light that sets
across Athens every night.'
The hotel's spa and gym contain the same vital but
easygoing colours. Orange dominates the gym, which is
dressed with wallpaper designed by Karim for Marburger
Germany, along with coloured glass and mirrors, and
lime and pink tiles. One of Karim's common complaints
concerns hotel gyms. He often encounters spaces that
aren't functional. In one São Paulo hotel, Karim worked
out in a room that had no illumination other than a
handful of blue LEDs. He couldn't see his diagnostics on
the treadmill. In the Semiramis, the spaces are bright and
simple. And small. With only 250 m² for gym, changing
rooms, showers, a steam room and two massage rooms,
Karim had to mete out real estate carefully. Not only did
he specify the equipment; he also designed bathrobes and
slippers, an LED message board stocked with inspiring
phrases, a centre island with refrigerated cold face towels
with energetic scents, a water and vitamin bar, and
packaging for the amenities. Continuing his pledge to
avoid hotel clichés, he walled the massage rooms in pink
glass for an atmosphere both extraordinary and practical.
The efficiency of the layout and the generosity of poolside
views from the gym generate a sense of energetic peace.
Karim's world-view, he says, was an integral part of
his very personal approach to the Semiramis. Karim
believes that the world has returned to sharing a single
global language – binary notation – which allows us
to communicate instantly over vast distances and is
shrinking the globe. Karim's theory is everywhere
apparent. In the Semiramis, there are no room numbers,
only symbols that the designer likens to contemporary
hieroglyphics. 'I believe my work is the study of
alternatives and possibilities,' he says. 'Products and
furniture must mediate between industry and the user,
between self-expression and desire, between production
technologies and human behaviour. I am an artist of real
issues.' The design of the Semiramis makes it clear: Karim
is in the process of producing a total work of art, but it
is a manifesto that is less about design than about rosy
optimism in a beige world.

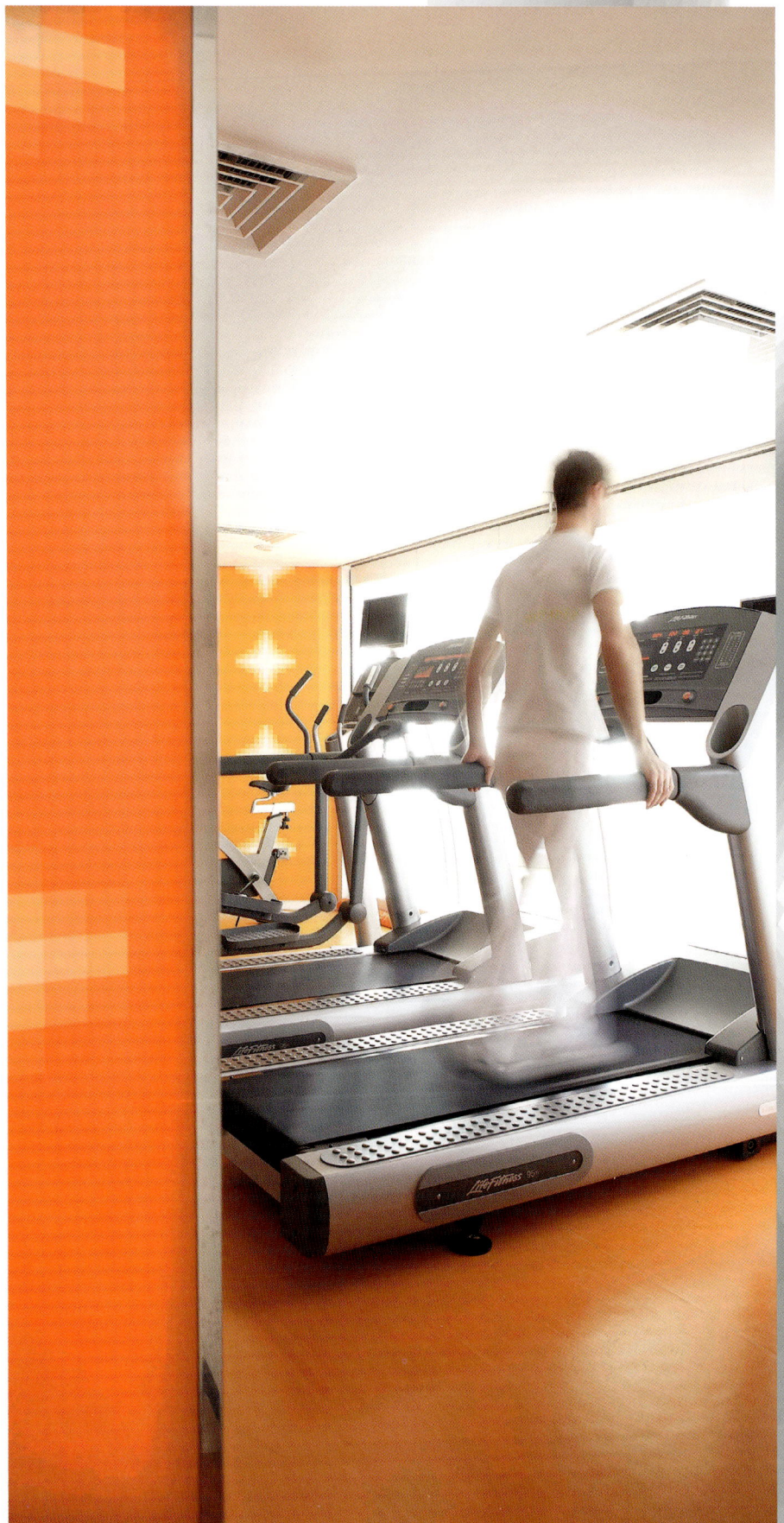

↑ Colours – here in the gym and
throughout the hotel – celebrate
energy and optimism.

→ Chartreuse balconies and a
terrace lounge in warm shades
of red overlook the pool,
which has an unusual bottom
striped with the colours of the
Mediterranean Sea.

'In the Semiramis, I have developed
my own little utopia'

«Karim Rashid»

Atop the roof, the pool's
amoeboid shape is repeated
in a coiling retaining wall and
in sloping ramps lined with
coloured glass balustrades. The
restaurant opens out onto a deck
and the pool below. 'I would live
there if I could!' Karim has said
of the Semiramis.

Karim designed virtually every
product in the hotel, from staff
uniforms and deck furniture to
gym benches and the slippers
available for patrons of the spa.

architect
Karim Rashid
357 West 17th Street
New York, NY 10011
USA
T +1 212 929 8657
F +1 212 929 0247
office@karimrashid.com
www.karimrashid.com

photographers
Jean-Francois Jassaud
luxproduction@wanadoo.fr
-
Vangelis Paterakis
fotopaterakis@ath.forthnet.gr

legend
01 Gym
02 Sauna
03 Massage room
04 Showers
05 Lavatories
06 Storage

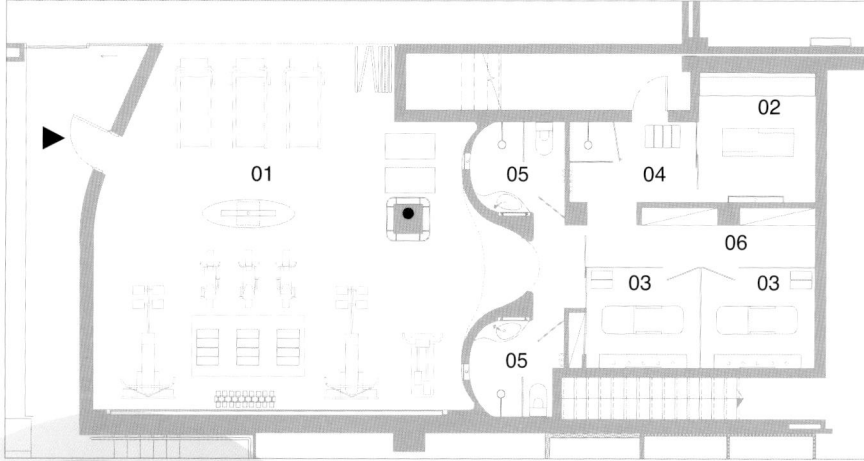

client
David Barton Gym
graphic design
Mathu Anderson
total floor area (m²)
9150
total cost (US$)
4 million

**duration of
construction**
6 months
opening
October 2005

project
David Barton Gym
600 West Chicago Avenue
Chicago, IL 60610
USA
T +1 312 836 9127
F +1 312 836 9174

gps
N 41°53' E -87°38'

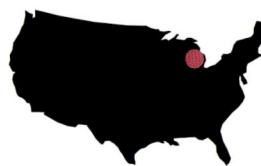

Studio Sofield

David Barton Gym

chicago/usa

Text by Tim Groen

Salvaged streetlights. Vintage seating by Niels Diffrient, Eames and Wendell Castle. An abstract mural comprising colourful Flokati rugs. A dramatic Chinese wedding bed set against a blow-up of smoky eyes. Just a few of the surprises which emerged from a David Barton-Studio Sofield collaboration that became the David Barton Gym in Chicago.

'I'm thrilled that my first foray into Chicago is part of the rebirth of Kingsbury Park,' says David Barton about his fifth gym. Experiencing a wave of redevelopment, Kingsbury Park is a former industrial area on the north side of Chicago, just across the Chicago River from the Loop. Following the pattern present in all his facilities, here, too, Barton has let the building inspire the design. 'All my gyms are different. They're an alternative to the chain movement,' says Barton, who fell in love with the monumental warehouse built in 1908. The area may belong to history, but today it's what Barton describes as 'a young, hip, loft neighbourhood'.

The fitness entrepreneur, who can hardly be accused of taking an obvious approach – whether in his advertising campaigns or his overall approach to urban fitness – hired New York-based Studio Sofield to turn 9150 m² of ground-floor space into a dramatic yet functional David Barton Gym. Sofield – a name linked for all eternity to the 400 Gucci boutiques that founder Bill Sofield designed at the height of Tom Ford's reign – maintained elements of the early 20th-century architecture of the former Montgomery Ward & Co. Catalog House overlooking the city's Riverwalk. Barton is pleased that Studio Sofield treated the gym as though it were a museum, 'paying homage to a classic, while creating a theatrical, visceral aesthetic to provide athletic inspiration'. Situated directly on the riverbank, the gym offers dramatic city views through its glass façade. The arched ceilings and octagonal terracotta columns are illuminated by clusters of Herzog & de Meuron lights.

Once Chicagoans flash their membership cards at the monolithic walnut reception desk, they find themselves in an entrance area dotted with an assortment of 20th-century classics; an Arco light, Eames chaises and a Vladimir Kagan sectional are all part of the assortment. A cartoonish, spun-steel Fireorb fireplace juts down from the ceiling, and its long black pipe serves as a graphic exclamation point in the open space. Outfitted with an LCD screen and looping continuous footage of flames, it leaves no question about its purely decorative purpose.

A spun-steel Fireorb fireplace juts down from the ceiling in the entrance area.

Another touch of drama is provided by an antique Chinese wedding bed, with an abundance of pillows tossed against the wall at its head. Through the posts and from under its canopy peek the smoky eyes of Barton's wife, nightlife doyenne Suzanne Bartsch. 'The Chinese bed is just like the one I sleep in at home,' says Barton. 'It's so unexpected, and it reminds people that they shouldn't take gym time too seriously.'

In the gym area, vintage touches include an early 20th-century scale and salvaged streetlights, here combined with GTM lighting. One wall is covered in a custom installation of dyed Flokati rugs. Besides providing colour and texture in a space dominated by grey, as well as by industrial materials, the fluffy rugs serve to muffle the noise in the work-out zone.

The cardiovascular area, with its rows of rows of machines paired with plasma-screen televisions, was positioned within the interior to get the most out of riverfront views. The core of the gym has been dedicated entirely to free weights and dumbbells, and Barton proudly points out that the facility features the most expansive collection of weight machines in Chicago – a statement that was certain valid at the time of opening. Three fitness rooms in the back include an indoor cycling studio and a 'yoga sanctum' furnished with Sacco beanbags for exhausted

bodies to sink into while recovering from more strenuous activities. Whereas most of the work-out area is tiled with (recycled) rubber flooring, Interface carpet tiles were selected for the yoga space.

Shower stalls separated by travertine marble are outfitted with oversized blade showerheads by Hans Grohe. The steam room is, in press-release speak, 'enlivened with a fibreoptic light experience'. Installed in the Russian bath are a river-rock floor and two-tiered teak benches. Walls and ceiling are lined in long, narrow, grey-slate tiles chosen for their heat-retaining properties.

The concept of creating a gym that offers more than a utilitarian work-out space, is derived from the classic Greek gymnasium, Barton says. The man is already working on another project with Studio Sofield for a branch to be located in a Miami Beach hotel. This one, he says, will be totally different, 'Upon entering, you walk into a round space with a ceiling over 12 m high. I really wanted to get away from minimalism in South Beach, so we're making the new gym sort of Moroccan flavoured.' Don't take that reference too literally, he warns, because 'it will still be done in the bad-ass, New York, punk-rock way that I do everything'.

↑ The work-out area is tiled with recycled rubber flooring.

→ The core of the gym has been dedicated to free weights and dumbbells.

The yoga room is furnished with Sacco beanbags for exhausted bodies to sink into while recovering from more strenuous activities.

The elegant locker rooms lead to the steam rooms and Russian baths.

'All my gyms are different; *they're an alternative to the chain movement*'

«David Barton»

↑ The entrance area leads to the monolithic walnut reception desk where the Chicagoans flash their memberships card to enter the gym.

→ Smokey eyes peek through the posts of the antique Chinese wedding bed.

interior designer
Studio Sofield
380 Lafayette St.
New York, NY 10003
USA
T +1 212 473 1300
F +1 212 473 0300
eoneill@studiosofield.com

photographer
Nathan Kirkman
www.nathankirkman.com

legend
01 Reception
02 Lounge
03 Stretching area
04 Strength-training area
05 Spinning room
06 Group-exercise room
07 Cardio room
08 Yoga room
09 Steam room

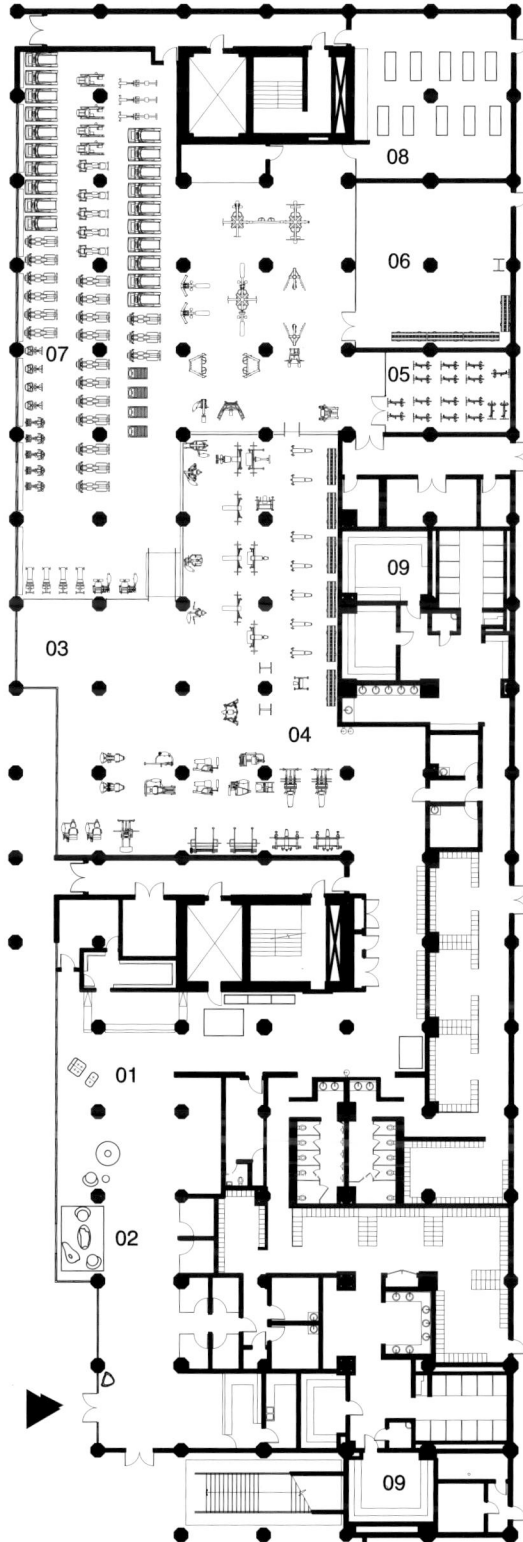

client
Gymbox
consultant
Light + Design Associates
engineer
Eckersley O'Callaghan
total floor area (m²)
1600
total cost (£)
2.2 million
budget per m² (£)
1375

duration of construction
4 months
opening
December 2006

project
Gymbox
Covent Garden
42-49 St Martin's Lane
London, WC2N 4EJ
UK
T +44 20 7395 0270
www.gymbox.co.uk

gps
N 51°30' E 00°7'

Ben Kelly Design

Gymbox

london/england

Text by Chris Scott

Breaking the mould of traditional sports centres, Gymbox – whose claim is that 'you will be part of a totally unique gym experience' – offers all the fun and excitement of a club. Keep fit, build the body, enjoy the buzz and thank Ben Kelly Design for the oh-so-cool surroundings.

Ben Kelly Design, well-known for the legendary Haçienda club in Manchester, England, was approached by the owners of Gymbox to design a second sports centre in central London as a follow-up to their Holborn facility. The rousing success of the first Gymbox, also by Ben Kelly Design, was the catalyst for the conversion of a venue in Covent Garden: a former art house, Lumiere Cinema, on St Martin's Lane known not only for its alternative films but also for its trendy clientele. Converting a cinema from the '60s into a destination marked by power and perspiration can also be seen as an alternative move. The brief asked for 'a stimulating and bold environment that would avoid the cliché of a fitness market saturated with white-box spaces'. The new design was to be a natural progression from the original Gymbox, yet with a slightly more sophisticated interior than its predecessor – a space in harmony with the luxurious establishment on the floors above: the St Martins Lane Hotel designed by Philippe Starck.

The Ben Kelly designers faced numerous challenges. For starters, the 1600-m² interior covers the ground floor and two lower levels. Accessibility proved difficult during the realization phase, as the main space is two levels below the ground-floor entrance. Getting mechanical systems into and out of the building was especially complicated,

for example. And the building's cinematic legacy had to remain intact, a precondition that necessitated preservation of the floor plan. It wasn't easy for the designers to introduce all the elements required to prepare the art house for its new role.

The entrance has retained its original canopy, and it's impossible to miss the bold lettering of the logo created by design agency Explosive. Once inside, visitors spot a 'what's on' cinema billboard that lists the activities taking place at Gymbox. An effort was made to keep – and where necessary to restore – as much as possible of the existing interior. The impressive terrazzo staircase and wall cladding in the main entrance lobby have survived the renovation. Unfortunately, the auditorium ceiling contained asbestos and had to be removed. Seizing this opportunity, the designers created a double-height space that corresponds to its new cultural form and function, while losing none of its dramatic feel.

A glass-fronted dance studio, suspended from the ceiling, has replaced the original projection screen. As the focal point of the interior, the studio is framed in fluorescent pink, and its glossy exterior reflects the frenetic activity around it. A live DJ in a club-like booth is positioned to one side of this volume. Another theatrical touch is a heavy yellow backdrop curtain by Kvadrat, strikingly

↑ An overall view of the facility features the dance studio, which hovers above the boxing ring, and a 'what's on' billboard that lists activities at Gymbox.

← A 'cinema-style' light box shows what's going on inside.

illuminated and stretching the full two floors.
Walkways made from perforated industrial-steel decking
– articulated with coloured linear lighting beneath the
surface – connect all higher elements. One original
stairway has been preserved, however, in homage to the
past.

All terraces and stairways end at a central point below the
suspended studio, where a collection of punchbags invites
budding athletes to enter a full-sized Olympic boxing ring.
Light+Design Associates created the overall lighting
scheme, which includes a clever mix of theatrical
spotlights that generate a sense of being 'on show'. An
illuminated display board announces the club's upcoming
programme. Living up to a reputation built largely on
clear, clean design and bold graphics, Ben Kelly has made
it easy for fitness enthusiasts high on energy to find their
way around.

Changing rooms or 'blocks', as they are called at Gymbox,
are housed in two stacked volumes juxtaposed at
opposite angles at the rear of the space. Floors made of
Dalsouple rubber feature broad diagonal stripes, and
rows of gleaming lockers sport reflective doors. Toilets
and showers exhibit a cool array of rectangular tiles
in basic black, white and grey. Vertical and horizontal
stripes combined with shower stalls in coloured glass give
these areas a very graphic look. It's all very functional
– bordering on the industrial, perhaps – but the resulting
ambience is *haute design*.

Gymbox caters for a younger clientele that likes mixing
fitness with fun. While the DJ pumps up the excitement,
down-to-earth patrons work out and daredevils go in for
activities like 'Gladiator Games' and 'Bitch Boxing'. All this
combined with VPTs (Very Personal Trainers) and state-
of-the-art fitness equipment makes Gymbox one of the
hottest hang-outs in London's West End.

It's all very functional – bordering on the industrial, perhaps – but the resulting ambience is *haute design*

↗ Cinematic touches enhance a
   dimly lit corridor that leads to
   the action.

→ Theatrical illumination sheds
   light on the very latest in sports
   equipment.

Stairways and walkways take you straight to the heart of the gym.

architect
Ben Kelly Design
10 Stoney Street
London SE1 9AD
UK
T +44 20 7378 8116
T +44 20 7378 8366
info@bkduk.co.uk
www.benkellydesign.com

photographer
Philip Vile
www.philipvile.com

legend
01 Changing room
02 Studio 01
03 Studio 02
04 Studio 03
05 Projection screen
06 Upper Mezanine
07 Lower Mezanine
08 Cardio platform
09 Resistance platform
10 Free weights platform
11 The pit - abs/cardio
12 Boxing ring
13 Punchbag area
14 Sauna
15 Showers
16 DJ
17 Office

Ground floor

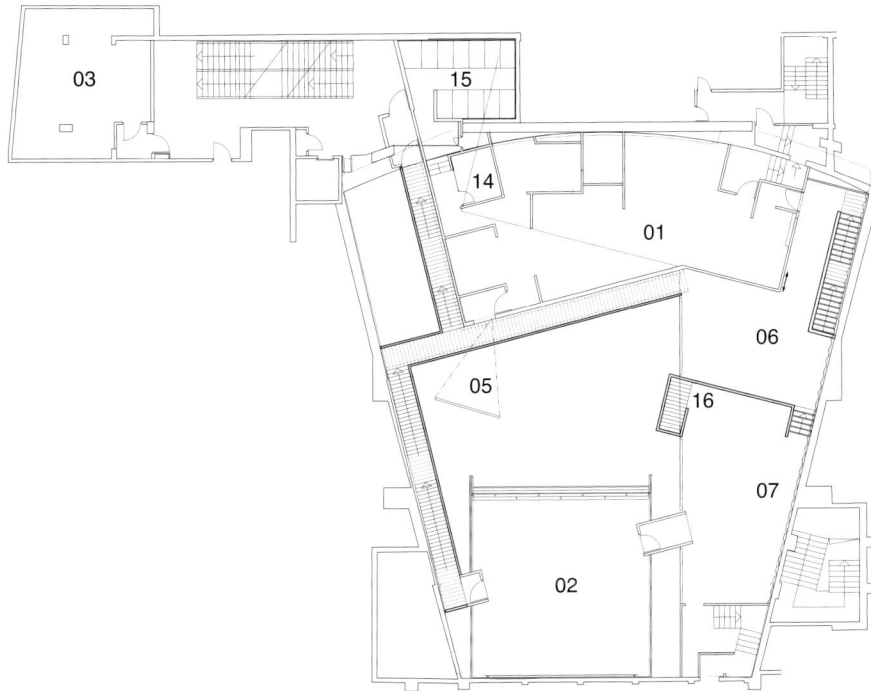

Basement

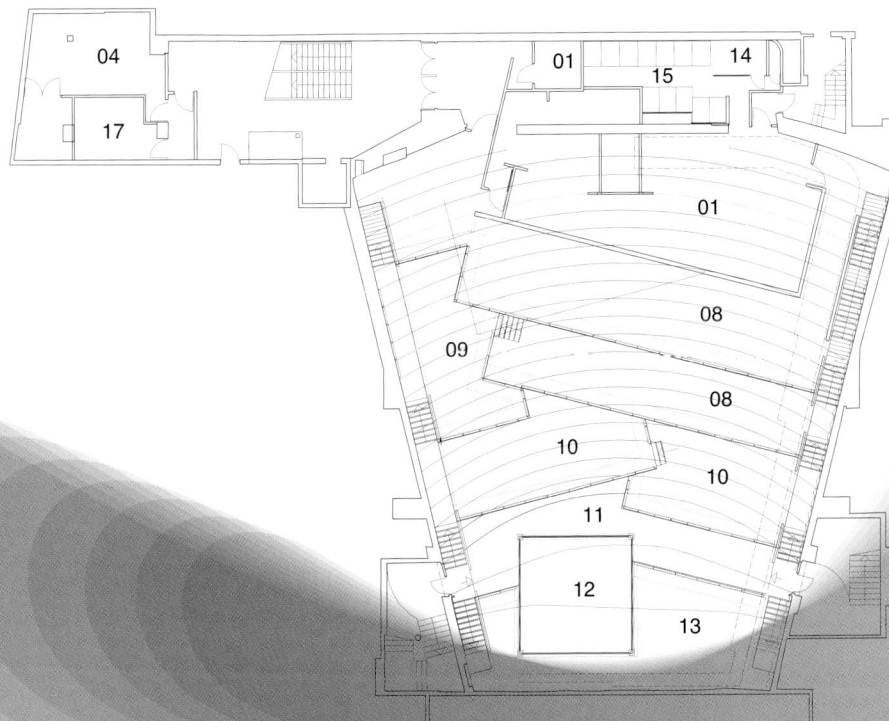

↖ Reflections are everywhere
   you turn in the smart changing
   rooms.

← The linear patterns and subdued
   tones of the tiling give toilets and
   showering facilities a seriously
   stylish look.

233

client
Mr. Vidur Sodhani and
Mr. Sjouke-Jan Zwarthoff
consultant
Ansorg
manufacturers
SB Constructions and The
Designo International
graphic design
Atelier René Knip
total floor area (m²)
400

total cost (€)
400,000
budget per m²
1000
**duration of
construction**
5 months
opening
September 2006

project
Elemention Health & Sport
Infinity Tower C,
Ground Floor
DLF Cyber City, DLF Ph-2
New Delhi, Gurgaon 122002
India
T +91 12 4414 7400
infinity@elemention.com
www.elemention.com

gps
N 28°39' E 077°6'

I+M Architects

Elemention Health & Sport

new delhi/india

Text by Joeri Bruyninckx

In September 2006, the Elemention Health & Sport fitness centre opened in New Delhi, the first of a chain of centres to be located throughout India. The Indian-Dutch partnership that initiated the project commissioned a Dutch firm, I+M Architects, to design the complex, which was to occupy the ground floor of a new office building in the explosively growing commercial heart of the city.

It's no surprise to find a wellness centre and gym surrounded by office buildings. An increasing number of international businesses include the employee's wellbeing in their corporate philosophy. After all, no one benefits from a tired and dejected workforce. In the rat race that passes for our world economy, health and energy have become so vital that 'survival of the fittest' can be taken almost literally. Elemention Health & Sport is intended as a place of relaxation and a gathering hole for expats, managers and staff members working in New Delhi-based companies, many with roots in Western countries. It is this concept that determined the priorities of the brief handed to I+M Architects: design a centre in which physical exertion and mental relaxation, wellness and sport, complement each other, while creating an ambience that is more European than Indian. The result is a concept, say I+M's designers, that attempts to bridge the 'often enormous differences between wellness centres and fitness clubs: an "oasis of relaxation" versus a "fitness factory".

We brought the two together in a playful space that invites guests to enjoy exercise.'
To achieve their goal, they avoided stationary walls wherever possible and made the central area a large, open space. In places requiring extra privacy, such as aerobics room and spas, they installed long, semi-transparent glass walls to separate these facilities from the central area. Like the large tinted windows on the other side of the space, these walls physically conceal certain zones while preserving an overall sense of openness. The designers accomplished the same objective with the strategic placement of elements such as strength and cardio equipment, offices, bar and reception; the zones thus created interconnect fluidly. This 'units on an open floor' principle allowed the designers to fit each component into the environment where it belonged. 'The concept had to be scaleable in order to adapt to a wide range of requirements. In a domestic environment, for example, there's more need for an aerobics room then for free weights.'

↑ Surprisingly, the only XL mirror in the interior is on a wall of the aerobics room. 'At Elemention, it's not about muscles and mirrors, but about feeling good.'

← The massage, changing and steam rooms are all finished in the same shade of pastel green, from glass mosaics on the walls to small tiles on the floors.

It is this flexibility in the design, along with the absence of conspicuous and unbalanced interventions, which exemplifies the European atmosphere the clients were so eager to have. Such an approach may suggest that the designers' signature is nearly invisible in this interior. But a well-organized interior and a subtle colour scheme are two things that I+M Architects try to inject into all their projects, regardless of genre – an aim that's a strong statement in itself. Certainly in the context of a fitness club, colour can actually sabotage the purpose of the activity – take pure white, for instance, or a brash colour meant to urge body builders to sweat up a storm. I+M's designers, however, used the same shade of grey-green in the wellness area for changing and massage rooms, plastered ceilings, tiled floor, and walls clad in glass mosaic tile. Various shades of white are found in both walls and ceilings of the fitness area, as well as in the glazed walls and birch Plexwood floor. Complementing the resulting fresh, serene atmosphere is a carefully chosen palette of warm, stimulating colours. Examples are the canary-yellow juice bar, which takes centre stage in the interior, and an orange practice floor visible through the glazed walls of the aerobics room.

A search for the right balance can also be seen in the use of textures and materials. Although Corian reception counter, glazed walls and gym floor flash a highly polished welcome, certain details have been deliberately given a somewhat coarser look. The relief on one wall of the aerobics room, for example, contrasts with the smooth practice floor, and strips of birch plywood on the juice bar give the vertical planes of this volume an unusual texture. The pronounced location of this bar – central and provocative – illustrates, for that matter, the Elemention Health & Sport philosophy. 'Naturally, the social function of the gym – the club feeling – is important. Seen from this perspective, the juice bar plays an important role.' Remarkably, the designers have excluded the customary floor-to-ceiling mirrors from this interior. Other than in the aerobics room, guests are given little opportunity to wallow in self-admiration while working out. 'Ultimately, it's not about muscles and mirrors, but about feeling well.'

An increasing number of international businesses include the employee's wellbeing in their corporate *philosophy*

Various shades of white in the central area conjure up a sense of serenity. Each element of the interior is indicated by a distinctive yet simple graphic symbol.

237

I+M insisted on a flexible
concept featuring a layout that
can be adapted to the client's
future wishes, whatever they may
be. The yellow juice bar draws
all eyes, even when viewed from
outside the building.

Semi-transparent glass walls
separate facilities such as
aerobics room and spas from the
central gym. Warm colours and
a wide range of materials add a
touch of spice to an otherwise
placid atmosphere.

architect
I+M Architects
Buyskade 39F
1051 HT Amsterdam
Netherlands
T +31 20 4861 685
im-ontwerpers@planet.nl
www.ina-matt.com

photographer
I+M Architects
Arjan Benning
www.arjanbenning.com

legend
01 Reception
02 Changing room
03 Health check
04 Strength area
05 Cardio area
06 Aerobics area
07 Steam room
08 Massage room
09 Juice bar
10 Storage

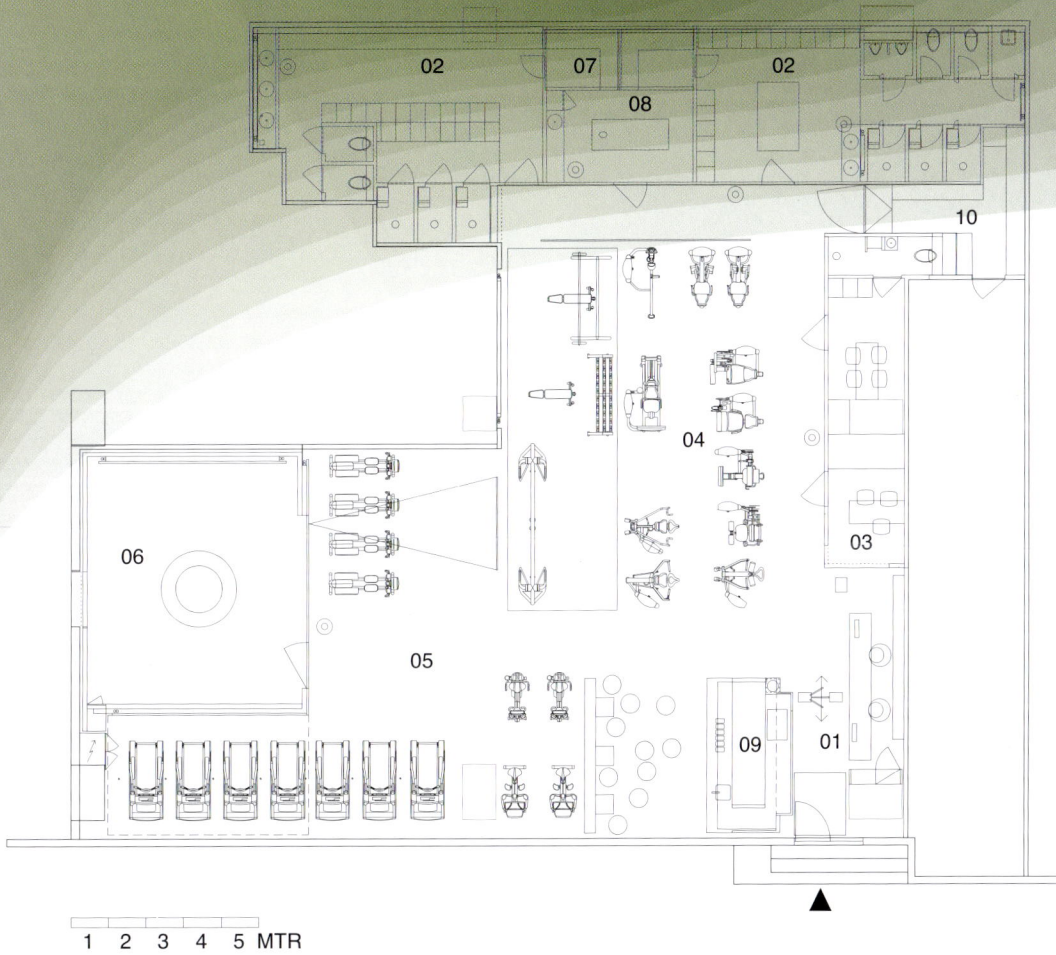

1 2 3 4 5 MTR

client
Mars Entertainment Group
engineers
Ata Muhendislik, Erguven
Insaat and Klimak Taahhüt
manufacturers
Props, Orka Dekorasyon,
Hayat Mobilya, Cukurcuma,
Idem Reklam and Mavi
Pencere
graphic design
Zebra Design Factory
lighting consultant
Van Lierde J.

**communication
and pr agency**
bernaylafem
total floor area (m²)
5189
total cost (US$)
6 million
**duration of
construction**
5 months
opening
April 2007

project
Mars Athletic Club/ NuSpa
Kanyon Shopping Mall
Buyukdere Cad. No.185
1.Levent
34394 Istanbul
Turkey
T +90 212 323 0999
F +90 212 323 1023
mackanyon@
marsathletic.com
www.marsathletic.com

gps
N 41°4' E 029°0'

Geomim
Mars Athletic Club/ NuSpa
istanbul/turkey

Text by Chris Scott

Mars Athletic Club and NuSpa are part of the Mars Entertainment Group, which was founded in 2000. The group, which caters to the upper end of the entertainment business, operates restaurants, bars, cafés and cinemas. Fitness facilities in Istanbul – know informally as MAC – represent a more recent addition.

The guys and gals who work out at the Mars Athletic Club have swapped the old 'no pain, no gain' cliché for the more cheerful 'no fun, we're done'. At MAC, the aim is to combine exercise and entertainment. The first MAC club – called MAC Kanyon because it's part of the Kanyon Shopping Mall in central Istanbul – opened in April 2007. Put together on a budget of 6 million dollars, this is a serious fitness facility that offers its clientele the whole works and then some. As efficient as a factory, the multifaceted complex has areas in which to sweat, swim, eat, drink, party, lounge and be pampered. It includes an outdoor terrace, valet parking, concierge service – even a place to have your laundry done!

For this specific operation, the Mars Entertainment Group approached design firm Geomim, one of Turkey's leading architecture and interior-architecture practices. Designer Mahmut Anlar, a cofounder of Geomim, stresses that the company has an ongoing philosophy based on several essential criteria: the pursuit of minimalist design in combination with a style that radiates quality, an interpretation of the future in the light of the past and the present, and a refusal to compromise on the fundamental principles of modern architecture. He and his team use the latest technologies wherever possible to create timeless designs. All these factors, combined with a disciplined approach to the work at hand, are responsible for Geomim's excellent reputation. To realize MAC Kanyon, the designers worked in close collaboration with the entertainment group. The main goal was to produce a club that would provide 'more than a work-out session' and that would 'generate the feeling that the customer has escaped the chaos of the city and has gone on holiday for a couple of hours'.

Spread over three floors, the club has an overall surface area of 5189 m² – quite a bit of space, but a lot had to be fitted into these premises. The designers were delighted to be able to 'bring sport out into the daylight', as gyms in Turkey are generally located underground. From the

The open stair-way at the Kaucuk Juice Bar leads to serious sporting activities.

beginning, it was evident that MAC would be like no other sporting facility in the city. The entrance – marked by giant doors – is at ground level, as is the centrally positioned Kaucuk Café, which boasts specially designed furniture, the work of interior designer Deniz Duru and Geomim's interior designer, Sinan Erul. Although Kaucuk's motto is 'eat well,' the café is not only a place to have a meal, but also a social hub, complete with a mobile DJ to liven up the crowd with musical entertainment. So far, not much physical exercise . . .

After coffee and a chat, however, patrons move up to the first floor – by means of an industrial-style hydraulic lift or, more appropriately, the open stairwell – where they check in at reception and get ready to work out. The next stop is a checkup where physical conditions are monitored. Having been told that all systems are go, they proceed to the 1000-m^2 cardio and weights area, where daylight streams in from three sides. Here they find a fantastic array of fitness equipment, including a ski and snowboard slope covered in synthetic grass that permits the user to enjoy a view of Istanbul while practising on the piste.

Graphic work by Zebra Design Factory – an outfit that regularly creates graphics for the Mars Entertainment Group – can be found on all three levels. Zebra expressed its interpretation of the MAC customer – 'a sexy, slightly zany person who's into fitness' – on the walls of the club in cool, attractive and energetic images. Key colours are red, black, grey and white, a palette that recurs throughout MAC Kanyon.

The second floor is no disappointment either. Here, a Pilates studio shares the space with stylish blocks of 'graphic' lockers and, even more important, the ultimate spa experience at NuSpa. This contemporary version of the traditional spa – far away from the bustle and activity of the café and the exercise areas – resembles an oasis of quiet and calm, with its décor of predominantly black laminated walls, lighting fixtures and white PVC-clad floor. Chestnut furniture, among which the very attractive massage tables, was designed by Deniz Duru. This restful retreat – where you can hear yourself breathing, feel your senses slip beyond all boundaries, mentally enter a place where you become someone else – lends access to the lap pool and to the 700-m^2 sunbathing terrace on the first floor.

A second MAC / NuSpa, designed by Creative Architecture, has opened in Club Resort Select Maris in Marmaris, and plans are under way for future MAC facilities in Ankara, Izmir and Istanbul, all to be designed by Geomim.

At MAC, the aim is to *combine exercise and entertainment*

Choose between the pool or gym facilities for a good work-out.

At MAC, a fresh interpretation was brought to the sauna and the modern-day Turkish baths.

architect
Geomim
Mahmut Anlar and
Sinan Erul
Tesvikiye Cad. Dilek Apt.
No.95, K.1 D.5 Tesvikiye
80200 Istanbul
Turkey
T +90 212 236 5704
F +90 212 236 5804
geomim@geomim.com
www.geomim.com

photographer
Yavuz Draman
yavuz@yavuzdraman.com
www.yavuzdraman.com

legend
01 Reception
02 Changing room
03 Studio
04 Gym
05 Pilates room
06 Kinetic-exercise room
07 Snowboard area
08 Basketball area
09 Pool
10 Steam room
11 Massage room
12 Turkish bath
13 Sauna
14 Showers
15 Lounge
16 Kaucuk Café
17 Terrace
18 Toilets
19 Office

Second floor

Ground floor

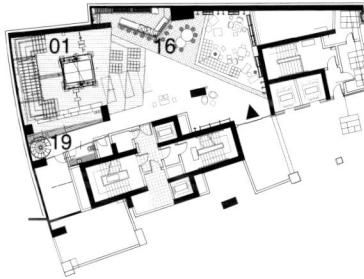

First floor

↖ NuSpa offers massages in a dark, quiet and calm ambience.

← View from above: the Kaucuk Café

← The changing rooms are designed to create an industrially hygienic, relaxing atmosphere.

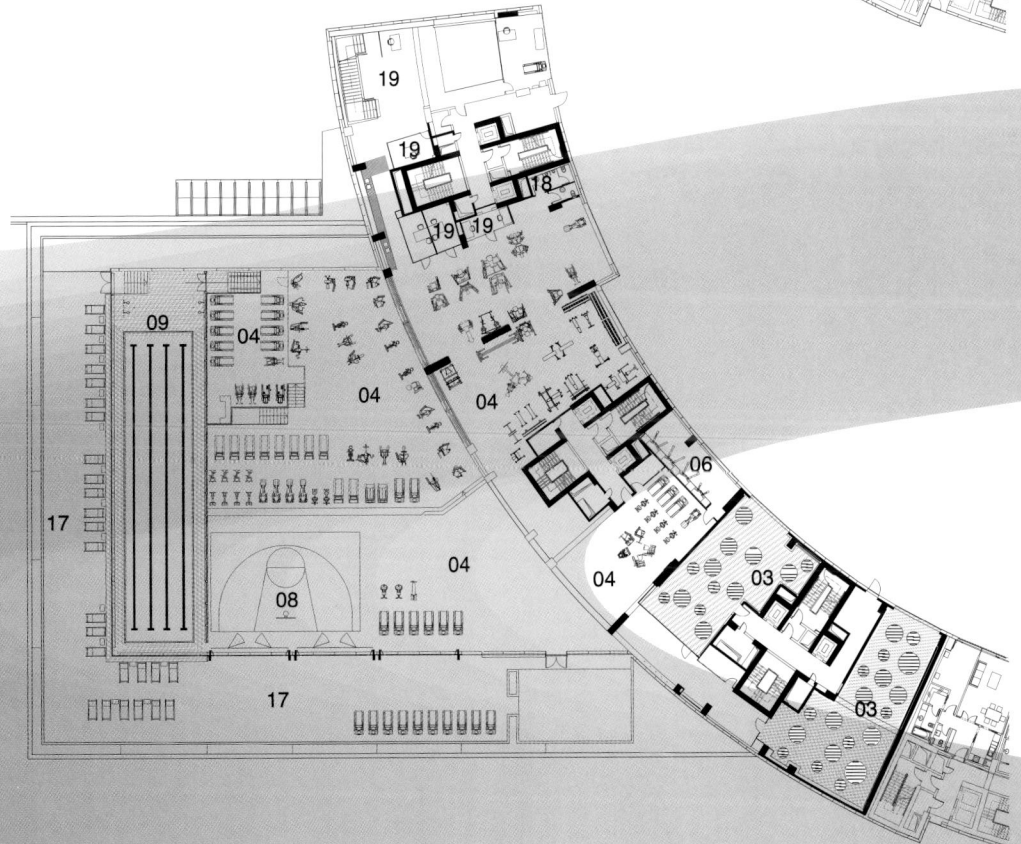

249

client
City of New York
consultant
MIT Media Lab
equipment brands
WaterRower, Reebok,
LifeFitness, Precor,
Nautilus, Vision and
Bowflex

capacity
30 clients
total floor area (m²)
610 - 1220
opening
2008

gps
N 40°42' E -74°0'

Terreform
River Gym
new york/usa

Text by Tim Groen

'Why should gym members be forced to stare at a mirror, television or static streetscape when their entire body is active?' That was the question that motivated Mitchell Joachim of New York-based Terreform to design a series of capsular floating gyms that run on energy derived from human motion. 'Human power is green power.'

Terreform, defined on its website as a 'design collaborative that integrates ecological principles in the urban environment', approaches ecology in design as 'a focused scientific endeavour'. Solutions by this not-for-profit organization include 'urban self-sufficiency infrastructures, climatic tall buildings, and smart mobility vehicles for cities'. In 2005 Terreform's Mitchell Joachim, principal architect of Archinode Studio, and personal trainer Douglas Joachim entered *New York Magazine*'s Create a Gym competition with a design that literally took the work-out crowd out of their glass-and-carpet boxes. According to judge and fitness mogul David Barton, who declared their entry one of the top three designs, the proposal 'poetically harnesses energy directly from the human buttocks'.

By envisioning work-out facilities as a flotilla of bubble-like vessels that travel circuitously along New York City's Hudson and East Rivers, the designers have arguably overstepped the boundaries of what is commercially realistic. But whether the concept is realistic or not, Terreform expanded it even further by making exercisers the source of energy for their own gym. The average exercise performed using industrial fitness equipment consists of controlled, repetitive, single-plane movements. 'All of this energy is summarily dissipated and ultimately exhausted for the sake of a single individual's wellbeing,' reasons Joachim. 'Other potentials exist to harness this vast human expenditure of caloric energy.' Since the River Gym is to be outfitted with water-purification devices to help alleviate pollution levels in the waters around Manhattan, and since the vessels will ultimately transport 'less-motivated citizens' as well, the River Gyms will not only create a unique experience for the fitness crowd, but also serve the greater good.

Revolving on a computer-navigated river loop averaging around 15 minutes – a route that connects to selected points in Brooklyn, Staten Island and New Jersey – the soft 'micro-islands' that make up the River Gym flotilla have the potential to ease the burden on the city's ferry lines during peak hours. The local water-taxi market has shown serious interest in the concept, which is not surprising considering that a substantial amount of new real estate is built on, or near, Manhattan's waterfront. Although the new waterfront properties are desirable and popular, the downside is that residents will have to wait for subway expansion. An accessible mode of transportation that

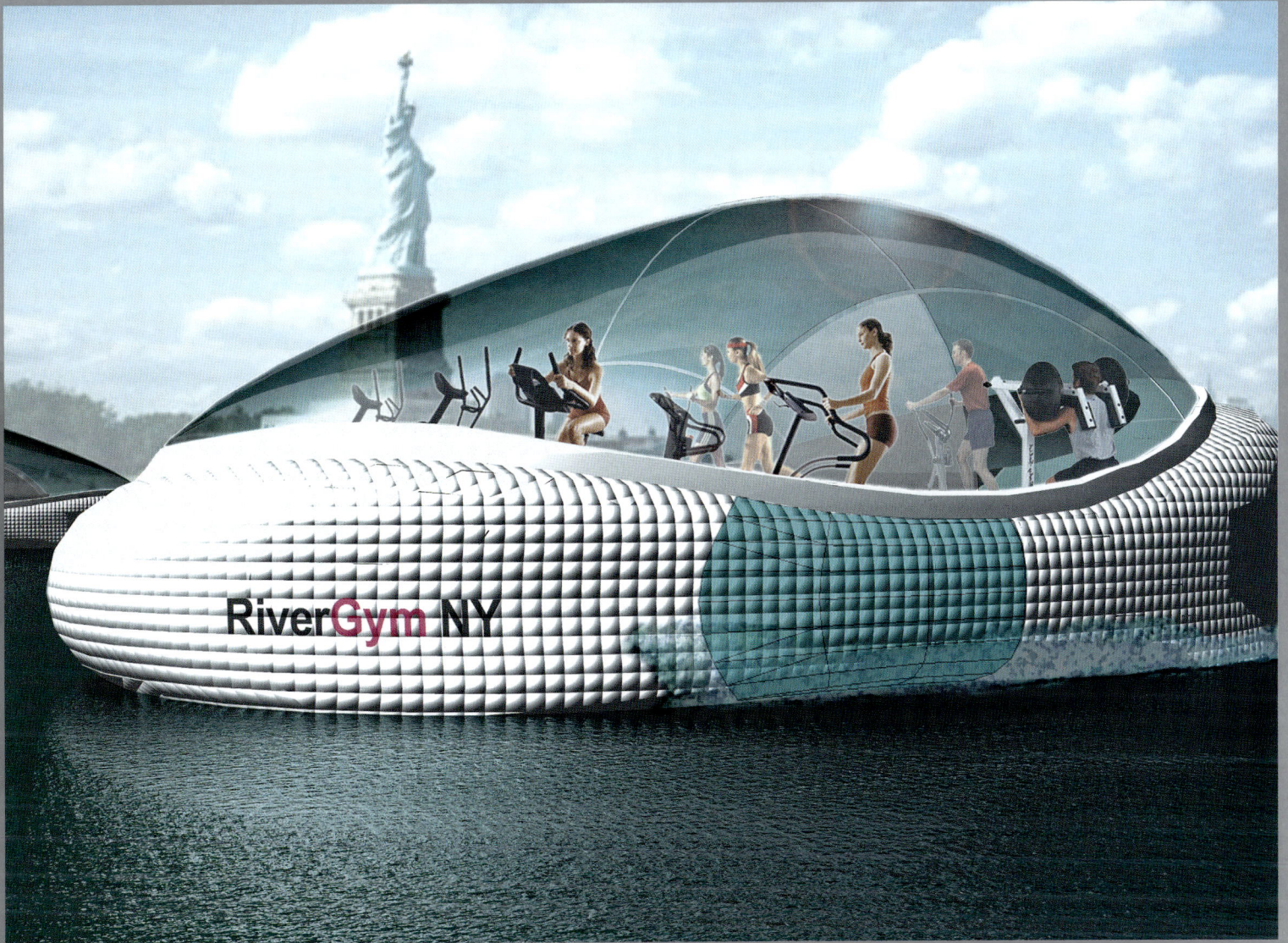

↑ Let's get physical: up to 30 passengers can board a River Gym vessel for an unusual commute, as long as a certain number of them are willing to work out for the duration.

← Beneath the craft's rounded shell, which consists of a soy-based plastic, are foil-pillow walls and other components made from recycled materials.

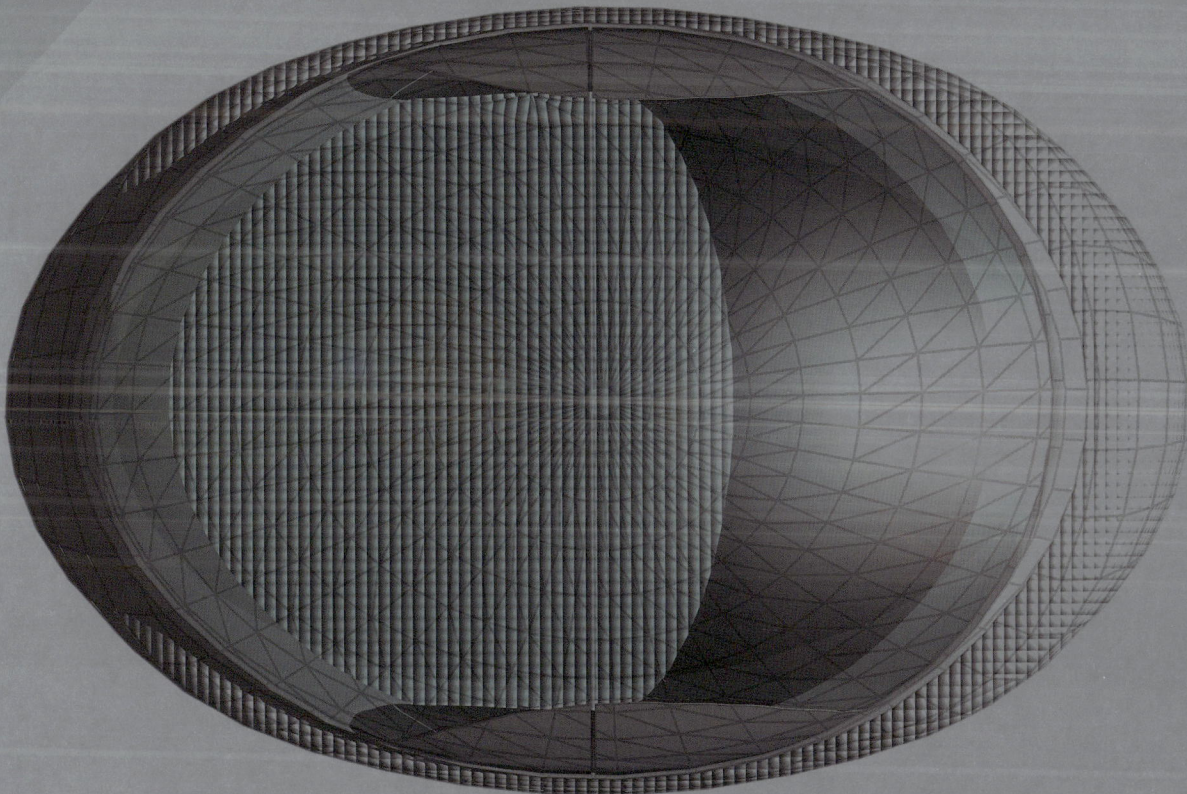

can kill two birds with one stone is sure to appeal to the athletically inclined. 'The idea is that you can easily access your River Gym vessel,' say the designers, 'to travel to and from multiple points in the city.' Extra passengers on board can actually benefit the exercisers; passengers increase the vessel's mass and amplify the intensity of the exercise. Because these vessels vary in size, some need only a few passengers to boost the energy level of the craft, while larger ones are reserved for peak hours. Passengers and gym members can sign in and board at a number of modest docking facilities along the riverbanks. These points of departure feature reception desks, locker rooms, health-food kiosks and all the other amenities expected of a modern work-out facility.

The 610- to 1220-m^2 River Gyms, which are designed for a maximum capacity of 30 passengers each, are to be built using recycled wood and plastic composite timber. Topping the gym's foil-pillow walls is a transparent, soy-based plastic shell. 'This is the kind of munificent vision for which the great city of New York is renowned,' is Terreform's view of the utopian proposal, which is intended to redefine the urban gym in a cost-effective and environmentally friendly manner.

↑ New York City's recent crop of waterfront properties is in high demand, but public transport serving such areas is not always a reality. River Gym offers a solution to the New Yorker who opts for a lifestyle without a car in the garage.

→ Designed to link several Manhattan locations to points in Brooklyn, Staten Island and New Jersey, River Gym provides an alternative to rush-hour ferry commutes.

Human power is *green power*

architect

Mitchell Joachim, Ph.D.,
and Douglas Joachim
180 Varick Street #930,
New York, NY 10014
USA
T +1 212 627 9120
mj@archinode.com
www.archinode.com and
www.terreform.org

Project locations

062 TOKYO-JP

078 TOKYO-JP

140 TOKYO-JP

164 TOKYO-JP

172 TOKYO-JP

202 TOKYO-JP

124 KUWANA-JP

108 OSAKA-JP

156 TAIPEI-TW

186 HONG KONG-CN

218 CHICAGO-US

250 NEW YORK-US

092 SANTA MONICA-US

148 NEW YORK-US

asia

062 ému
    assistant
078 Caon Toyosu
    TONERICO:INC.
108 Glamour Annex
    Propeller Design
156 Aesop
    – Breeze Centre
    CJ Studio
124 Edge Lotus Beauty
    Salon
    Hiroshi Nakamuro
140 Xel-Ha by afloat
    Jun Aoki & Associates

164 LIM Hair clinie
    Isolation Unit
172 Asta Aveda
    Curiosity
186 Yoga Plus
    Cream
202 Illoiha Ebisu and
    Omotesando
    Tokyo/Japan
234 Elemention Health
    & Sport
    Nendo

usa

092 Dermalogica on
    Montana
    Abramson Teiger
    Architects
148 The House of Bumble.
    Anderson Architects
218 David Barton Gym
    Studio Sofield
250 River Gym
    Terreform

legend
● Spas
● Salons
● Gyms

054 AMSTERDAM-NL

014 INNSBRUCK-AT

038 PARIS-FR

022 BASEL-CH

030 BADEN-CH

132 BASEL-CH

116 BARCELONA-ES

226 LONDON-UK

194 COLOGNE-DE

070 BERLIN-DE

006 LANGENLOIS-AT

046 VIENNA-AT

086 ALGÕ-HU

100 VIENNA-AT

242 ISTANBUL-TR

210 ATHENS-GR

234 NEW DELHI-IN

colophon

**Relax
Interiors for
Human Wellness**

publishers
Frame Publishers
www.framemag.com,
Birkhäuser Verlag AG
Basel · Boston · Berlin
www.birkhauser.ch

compiled by
Sarah Schultz

introduction by
Karim Rashid

text by
Anneke Bokern, Joeri
Bruyninckx, Tim Groen,
Sarah Martín Pearson,
Shonquis Moreno, Stephan
Ott, Chris Scott and Masaaki
Takahashi

graphic design
Smel, Amsterdam
www.smel.net

copy editing
Donna de Vries-Hermansader

translation
InOtherWords
(D'Laine Camp, Donna de
Vries-Hermansader),
Ella Wildridge

sponsor
Klafs Saunabau GmbH &
Co. KG
www.klafs.de

colour reproduction
Neroc VGM, Amsterdam

printing
D2Print, Singapore

distribution
ISBN 978-90-77174-10-4
Frame Publishers
Lijnbaansgracht 87, 1015 GZ
Amsterdam, Netherlands
www.framemag.com

ISBN 978-3-7643-8392-3
Birkhäuser Verlag AG
Basel · Boston · Berlin
PO Box 133, CH - 4010
Basel, Switzerland
Part of Springer
Science+Business Media
www.birkhauser.ch

© 2007 Frame Publishers
© 2007 Birkhäuser Verlag AG

Library of Congress Control
Number: 2007931276

Die Deutsche
Nationalbibliothek
lists this publication in
the Deutsche National-
bibliografie; detailed
bibliographic data is
available in the internet
at http://d-nb.de